THE BASICS

This compact introduction is the ideal primer for anyone looking for an accessible overview of the basic principles of psychology, the fascinating science of mind and behavior.

In everyday life we often ask why people act the way that they do, especially when we encounter or hear about puzzling behavior. *Psychology: The Basics* introduces everyday explanations of behavior, considering them through a psychological lens. Illustrating how behavior can be explained through fundamental psychological principles, the book covers the core areas of cognitive, developmental, and social psychology as well as behaviorism, the human brain, our emotions, personality and individual differences, and psychological disorders.

This book, which includes further reading in each chapter for those wishing to study more deeply, is the perfect easy-to-understand introductory text for students, teachers, health personnel, human resource managers, administrators, and anyone interested in the human mind and behavior.

Rolf Reber is a professor of cognitive psychology at the University of Oslo, Norway.

The Basics

The Basics is a highly successful series of accessible guidebooks which provide an overview of the fundamental principles of a subject area in a jargon-free and undaunting format.

Intended for students approaching a subject for the first time, the books both introduce the essentials of a subject and provide an ideal springboard for further study. With over 50 titles spanning subjects from artificial intelligence (AI) to women's studies, *The Basics* are an ideal starting point for students seeking to understand a subject area.

Each text comes with recommendations for further study and gradually introduces the complexities and nuances within a subject.

ACTING (SECOND EDITION)
BELLA MERLIN

ANIMAL ETHICS
TONY MILLIGAN

ANTHROPOLOGY OF RELIGION
JAMES S. BIELO

ARCHAEOLOGY (SECOND EDITION)
CLIVE GAMBLE

THE BIBLE AND LITERATURE
NORMAN W. JONES

BRITISH POLITICS
BILL JONES

CAPITALISM
DAVID COATES

CHAUCER
JACQUELINE TASIOULAS

CHRISTIAN THEOLOGY
MURRAY RAE

DISCOURSE
ANGELA GODDARD AND NEIL CAREY

EDUCATION RESEARCH
MICHAEL HAMMOND WITH JERRY WELLINGTON

FINANCE (THIRD EDITION)
ERIK BANKS

FINANCIAL ACCOUNTING
ILIAS G. BASIOUDIS

FOLKLORE
SIMON J. BRONNER

FORENSIC PSYCHOLOGY
SANDIE TAYLOR

GERONTOLOGY
JENNY R. SASSER AND HARRY R. MOODY

GENDER (SECOND EDITION)
HILARY LIPS

JAPAN
CHRISTOPHER P. HOOD

LANGUAGE (SECOND EDITION)
R. L. TRASK

MEN AND MASCULINITY
NIGEL EDLEY

MEDIA STUDIES (SECOND EDITION)
JULIAN MCDOUGALL AND CLAIRE POLLARD

MEDIEVAL LITERATURE
ANGELA JANE WEISL AND ANTHONY JOSEPH CUNDER

MODERNISM
LAURA WINKIEL

NARRATIVE
BRONWEN THOMAS

POETRY (THIRD EDITION)
JEFFREY WAINWRIGHT

POVERTY
BENT GREVE

For a full list of titles in this series, please visit www.routledge.com/The-Basics/book-series/B

PSYCHOLOGY

THE BASICS

Rolf Reber

LONDON AND NEW YORK

First published 2020
by Routledge
2 Park Square, Milton Park, Abingdon, Oxon OX14 4RN

and by Routledge
52 Vanderbilt Avenue, New York, NY 10017

Routledge is an imprint of the Taylor & Francis Group, an informa business

British Library Cataloguing-in-Publication Data
A catalogue record for this book is available from the British Library

Library of Congress Cataloging-in-Publication Data
A catalog record for this book has been requested

ISBN: 978-1-138-55225-8 (hbk)
ISBN: 978-1-138-55226-5 (pbk)
ISBN: 978-1-315-14804-5 (ebk)

Typeset in Bembo
by Apex CoVantage, LLC

To my wife Hélène

CONTENTS

PREFACE

On a daily basis, we see behavior that is puzzling – an aggressive young man, a girl afraid of dogs, students struggling at school, or couples not getting along in their marriage. We ask why people act as they do, especially if behaviors are disadvantageous.

This book looks at explanations for such behaviors from the different viewpoints of scientific psychology. We shall see that these viewpoints are quite similar to lay explanations we come up with in everyday life. In order to be a science, we not only need plausible explanations but also evidence from studies that reveal to what degree these explanations are accurate. I have seen it as my task not only to review which explanations fare best but also to discuss how psychologists think. Although I draw the picture of a science that has gathered many new insights during the last 150 years, the journey is not at its end. There are many sprouts of new theories and approaches I could not review in this short book – we do not know which ones will survive scientific scrutiny and which ones will not. However, I am sure that in 20 years a few of them will become essential to the scientific lore of psychology.

I would like to thank people who discussed the book idea with me. Beyond three anonymous reviewers of the book proposal and the editorial staff at Routledge, I thank in person those of my friends and colleagues who have read excerpts of the book: Alan Fiske, Evalill Bølstad Karevold, Tilmann von Soest, Michael Stausberg, and Erik Stänicke provided me with invaluable comments that helped improve the book; however, any mistakes and weaknesses remain my own. Finally, my wife Hélène read the whole book, improved its clarity, and added the index. To her I dedicate this book.

INTRODUCTION

WHY DO WE DO WHAT WE DO?

We sometimes hear news stories like the one about a young smoker at a subway station in Hamburg, Germany. When an employee told him that smoking was prohibited, the young man attacked and seriously injured him. When we hear such stories, we are not only repelled by such behavior but also ask, why did the young man do that? We may come up with various answers.

Possible explanations include that the young smoker has never received proper punishment for his earlier misdeeds; he might think that if he attacks people who reprimand him, nobody will dare reprimand him in the future; anger makes him aggressive; something is wrong with his brain; he is not mature enough; he was provoked by the employee's rebuke; he expresses that his life lacks meaning; unconscious conflicts from childhood make him aggressive; it is in his character; he has grown up in a neighborhood where violence is common; this is the way lower classes express their resentment against suppression; the arrangement of the stars at his time of birth was inauspicious; or he is tempted by the devil.

All these everyday explanations except the last two are acceptable for a psychologist. Astrology, which claims to predict character from the arrangement of the stars at birth, has no scientific basis. In one well-known study, astrologers were not able to predict character from horoscopes (Carlson, 1985). Astrology is unscientific because it is not *evidence based*; it lacks valid findings in support of its assumptions. Being based on evidence is a requirement for any practice derived from psychology. When it comes to God or the devil, these are supernatural forces that cannot be examined by means of science; they are a matter of personal belief. Assumptions derived from pseudoscientific practices and religious beliefs are therefore not included in *psychology*, which is the science of mind and behavior.

Table 0.1 depicts the main scientific approaches in psychology. The first column lists the aforementioned everyday explanations for why the young smoker attacked the subway employee. In fact, these everyday explanations correspond quite well to general scientific explanations – after all, the first scientists started from everyday explanations, and many of them turned out to have some truth. Laypeople may differ in their preferred explanations. Some may think aggression is "inherited" through genetic transmission, whereas others think that it is "bad upbringing" caused by one's environment. The question whether genes or the environment determine behavior is the *nature-nurture debate* in scientific psychology.

Another debate pertains to the role of character versus situation as a cause of behavior. Interestingly, laypeople in North America and Europe prefer explanations in terms of "character" and "personality" for the young smoker's aggression, whereas people from South and East Asia are more likely to think that a specific situation motivated the young man's attack, for example anger stemming from being rebuked or (if his friends were around) the opportunity to impress others. The difference between explanations in Western and Eastern cultures has parallels to the *person-situation debate* in psychology. In the remainder of the book, we encounter both the nature-nurture debate and the person-situation debate, and we review the evidence in favor and against the different positions.

For each scientific explanation depicted in the second column of Table 0.1, there is an approach in psychology, as depicted in the third column. When parents or policy makers encounter a problem like aggression, they want to bring about change. Interestingly, methods of intervention to change behavior (listed in the fourth column) depend on the scientific explanation of behavior and therefore on the approach. In our example at the beginning, when we think that the young man attacked the subway employee because he had never

Table 0.1 Everyday explanations, corresponding general scientific explanations, psychological approaches to explain behavior, and interventions; the chapter in which an approach or intervention is reviewed is given in parentheses

Everyday explanation	*General scientific explanation of behavior*	*Approach*	*Interventions*
Earlier aggression was not punished	Learning (classical and operant conditioning)	Behaviorism (1)	Behavioral therapy (8)
He thinks he can evade rebuke	Thoughts (cognition)	Cognitive psychology (2)	Cognitive therapy (8)
He is motivated by anger	Motivation and emotion	Motivation and emotion (3)	Emotion regulation training
Something is wrong with his brain or genes	Brain function; genes	Biological psychology (4)	Medical treatment
He is not mature enough	Developmental processes	Developmental psychology (5)	Training to build competences
It is in his character	Personality traits	Personality psychology (6)	Character education
He was provoked by the rebuke	Social processes	Social psychology (7)	Social competence training
He lacks meaning in life	Meaning in life	Humanistic psychology	Client-centered therapy (8)
Unconscious conflicts cause his aggression	Unconscious childhood experiences	Psychoanalysis	Psychoanalysis (8)
He has grown up in a neighborhood where violence was common	Group and culture	Community and cultural psychology	Interventions at community level
The way lower classes express their resentment against suppression	Oppression; power hierarchies	Critical psychology	Interventions at societal level

been punished, we are tempted to require that his behavior be punished. When we think that his aggression is caused by erroneous thoughts, we try to correct his thoughts.

The main approaches are each discussed in their own chapters, while other approaches will be mentioned in passing. The first two chapters follow the historical development from behaviorism to cognitive psychology. Many theories of motivation and emotion reviewed in Chapter 3 are inspired by the cognitive approach. Biological methods like brain imaging and genetics have complemented psychological methods in the last three decades, as discussed in Chapter 4. The final four chapters build on these basic approaches to introduce human development, personality, social psychology, and psychological disorders, including psychotherapeutic interventions.

We derived Table 0.1 from explaining the behavior of a young man who attacked a subway employee after a rebuke. Note that the approaches we discuss can explain various kinds of behaviors. For example, why does Liza fear dogs? Why is Nora so happy? Why did Adrian become an architect? Why is Joshua good at school, whereas George shows poor performance? How does little Emily learn to speak? Why is it so difficult to stop smoking? Why do students procrastinate? What are the reasons marriages succeed or fail? For all these questions, laypeople give various answers, and so do psychologists; each of these problems can be addressed by different approaches. Whereas laypeople often are satisfied when a claim is plausible, scientists need to support an explanation by evidence gathered through studies conducted with proper methods, such as experiments or field studies.

PSYCHOLOGY AS A SCIENCE

Aggression, happiness, and learning difficulties are complex phenomena. For this reason, critics of psychology thought for a long time that it is not possible to explore the human mind and behavior with scientific methods.

The German psychologist Hermann Ebbinghaus (1913/1885) was among the first to challenge the idea that it is impossible to study psychology with scientific methods. He examined the time course of forgetting. The problem is that many factors influence forgetting, making systematic study difficult. For example, whether learners remember or forget a fact depends on its importance, how often they have learned the fact, and the learners' prior knowledge about a topic. Ebbinghaus controlled these factors in his experiment by using meaningless syllables, like HAC, NIV, and DOF. He learned these syllables until he could reproduce them perfectly. He learned the syllable list again after various intervals, ranging from 20 minutes to 1 month. Ebbinghaus measured how much learning effort he saved. For example, when he needed 10 trials to learn the syllables to perfection the first time and 2 trials after 20 minutes, he saved 80 percent; when he needed 9 trials after 31 days, he saved 10 percent. He observed that the forgetting curve is steepest at the beginning and then flattens; he forgot most during the first 20 minutes (see Figure 0.1). This is the classical forgetting curve.

Ebbinghaus and his successors studied memory with meaningless syllables under highly controlled conditions in the laboratory. Beyond the forgetting curve, Ebbinghaus and his successors could discover various laws of memory. For example, the more items a person learns, the worse is her memory performance; or, the first items on a list are remembered best. This so-called *primacy effect* plays a role when we form a first impression about a person.

Practitioners often object that laboratory studies lack *ecological validity*; that is, they are not representative for memory in the real world where materials are meaningful and important. We would need *field studies* that measure memory in everyday life to get valuable information about the real world. Again, such a claim must be

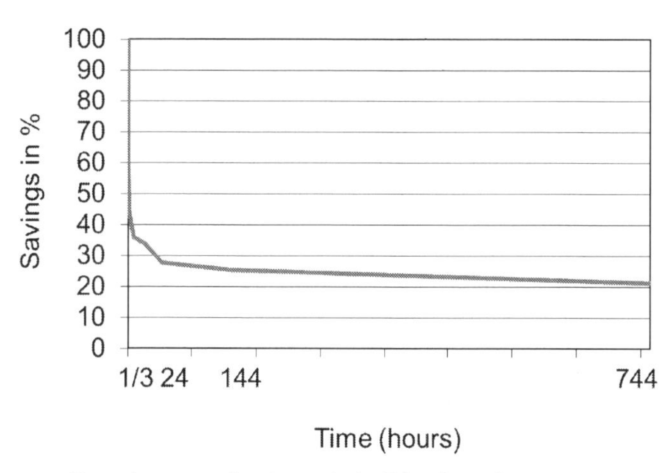

Figure 0.1 Forgetting curve after the results by Ebbinghaus. Savings is a measure of retention. Delays depicted on the *x*-axis are (from left to right) 20 minutes (1/3 hour), and 1, 6, and 31 days.

based on evidence. Let us look at heart resuscitation. Most people would agree that this is a meaningful and important skill that will be remembered for a long time after it has been learned. In order to test this assumption, McKenna and Glendon (1985) examined heart resuscitation skills of adults who attended a first aid course as part of their driving lessons. The tests were taken at different time points after the course, from 3 months to 3 years. The researchers tested four different criteria for memory of resuscitation skills: diagnosis, technique, performance, and the result as judged by an expert. As can be seen in Figure 0.2, even meaningful and important materials are subject to forgetting; the curves are similar to the forgetting curve in Figure 0.1.

The steep decline in remembering resuscitation techniques shows that **people forget skills when they rarely use them**, even when they might consider them important. However, learning a skill could be improved. Research in various domains suggests that the **best outcomes are seen with distributed learning**. In the case of resuscitation skills, distributed learning would mean that, for example, 6 months after the first aid course, the skill gets refreshed, and again after another year, and then after 2 years, and so on. With time, learners would forget less than after just one first aid course.

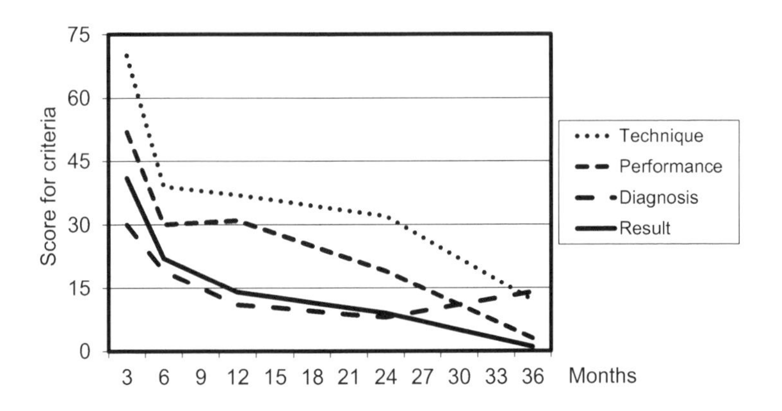

Figure 0.2 Memory for heart resuscitation skills

The study about resuscitation illustrates that controlled laboratory experiments often predict well what can be found in field studies. This is not only the case in studies on forgetting. In fact, correspondence between findings is high in those areas where sufficient numbers of both laboratory and field studies are available, such as memory, aggression, leadership style, helping behavior, and depression (Anderson, Lindsay, & Bushman, 1999).

The take-home message so far is that psychology is an empirical science based on evidence. Despite the complexity of human psychology, scientists were able to develop methods to study the mind and behavior, both in the laboratory and in the real world.

Recommended literature

Introductory textbooks in psychology review the topics covered in this book in more detail; a source for this book is:

Holt et al. (2015; see references).

LEARNING FROM EXPERIENCE

Behaviorism

In everyday language, we say that Liza avoids dogs because she fears them, or that the young smoker attacked the subway employee because he was angry. However, such parlance is problematic for the scientific study of behavior because we cannot observe internal states like fear or anger; we cannot look into the mind. What we can observe is behavior, such as avoiding dogs or attacking another person.

We might ask Liza whether she fears dogs or the young smoker whether he was angry when he attacked the subway employee. However, verbal reports about why people did something may be unreliable and (even worse from a scientific point of view) these reports cannot be confirmed by independent data; we simply have to believe what people tell us. Couldn't it be that Liza implies her fear of dogs from running away from them, or that the young aggressor says that he was angry in order to hide that he did it in cold blood?

As a response to the problems with self-reports, psychologists within an approach called *behaviorism* claimed that it is not possible to investigate mental states because there is no way to observe them. The best a researcher could do, they argued, is observe behavior. A scientist can objectively describe a *stimulus*, which is the object or event that elicits a behavioral response. Such a stimulus could be a dog, and the behavioral response running away or the facial expression of fear. However, the mental processes that connect the stimulus with the behavioral response – such as perception, categorization, memory, thoughts, intentions, and decisions – remain in the dark. The mind, according to behaviorists, is a black box that scientists are unable to open. Note that behaviorists restrict the scope of psychology. While the common definition of psychology emphasizes the study of both mind and behavior, behaviorists define psychology as the study of behavior.

Behaviorists explored learning. Commonly, we associate learning with school, where pupils learn mathematics or grammar that they have to retrieve at an exam. This is not what the behaviorists had in mind. They started from the assumption that organisms learn everything by experience. At birth, humans start with some basic reflexes, and learning builds on these reflexes. Behaviorists assumed that there are laws of learning that explain behavior, just as there are laws of physics that explain motion. They therefore searched for basic laws of learning.

The legacy of the behaviorists lies in their exploration of two main principles of learning – classical conditioning and operant conditioning – which are discussed in the next two sections. We conclude the chapter with a review of studies that revealed the limitations of behaviorism to explain human behavior. Despite its deficiencies, behaviorism discovered important principles of behavior analysis and behavior modification that have been applied in a variety of domains, most prominently in behavior therapy (see Chapter 8).

PAVLOV'S DOG: CLASSICAL CONDITIONING

Liza, a young woman, is frightened whenever she sees a dog. A common assumption is that prior experiences made Liza feel fear at the sight of dogs. We can try to disentangle the elements of this experience. Let us assume that as a child, Liza became frightened when a dog barked. As dogs often run towards a person and then bark, or wait until the person comes close enough before they bark, Liza had usually seen the dog before it barked. When seeing a dog often enough was followed by barking, Liza begins to show the fear response when she sees a dog, even if it does not bark.

Such learning from experience has been systematically studied since around 1900. The best-known study is commonly referred to as Pavlov's dog. Pavlov noted that dogs that were new to the experiment salivated when they saw the meat that the experimenter served them. However, after some time, dogs began to salivate when they saw just the experimenter. Pavlov, originally interested in the physiology of digestion, recognized that he might have found a fundamental learning principle. He just added a bell to his apparatus to examine this principle, which became known as *classical conditioning* or Pavlovian conditioning.

The experiment follows the logic shown in the four panels of Figure 1.1. (1) When a dog sees meat, it salivates. (2) When it hears the bell ringing without meat, it does not salivate. (3) The bell-ringing is paired with the meat; just before the dog gets the meat, the bell rings. Again, the dog salivates when it sees the meat. (4) After the animal goes through repeated trials where the ringing bell is paired with meat, the experimenter rings the bell but does not serve meat. Although the dog does not see meat, it salivates again.

There are four elements in this experiment: (1) meat, (2) bell-ringing, (3) salivation after seeing meat, and (4) salivation after bell-ringing alone. Meat is a stimulus that naturally elicits salivation as response. Meat is therefore the *unconditioned stimulus* (US) and the ensuing salivation is the *unconditioned response* (UR). Bell-ringing

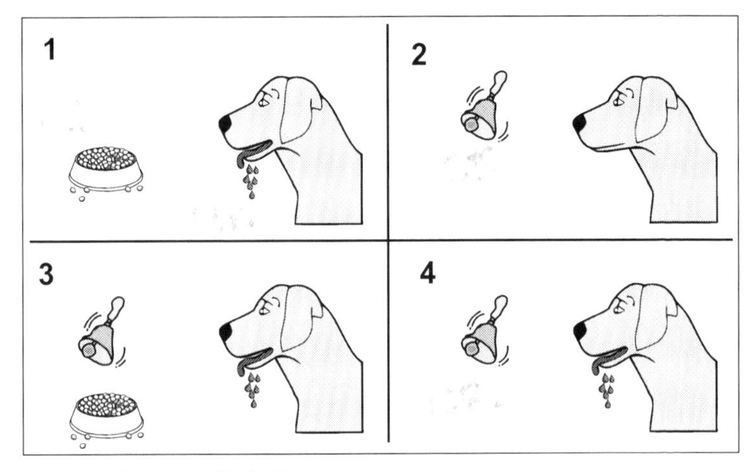

Figure 1.1 The setup of Pavlov's experiment

alone only elicits salivation after repeated pairings with the food. The effect of the bell is hence conditioned on being paired with the UR, in this case meat. Therefore, bell-ringing is the *conditioned stimulus* (CS) and salivation after bell-ringing without meat is the *conditioned response* (CR). It is worth pausing a moment to memorize these terms that are central to the understanding of the principles discussed next.

In the case of Liza, the sight of the dog is the CS and the barking the US. Fear as a response to barking is the UR, and fear as a response to the sight of the dog alone after repeated exposure to barking is the CR.

The acquisition phase often includes dozens of repeated pairings of CS and US before the CS elicits the CR. Therefore, bell-ringing has to be paired with meat repeatedly before the bell alone elicits salivation. Timing of pairings is crucial. Let us look at four different schedules.

The most efficient timing is to present the CS just before the US. In this case, the CS *predicts* the occurrence of the US and produces the strongest CR. In Pavlov's experiment, the bell rang and the dog received food within 2 seconds.

When the CS appears a long time before the US, the connection becomes weaker or disappears completely. When the bell rings 30 seconds before the meat is served, the dog attends to other stimuli in the environment and does not connect the ringing of the bell with the food. In fact, the coming of the experimenter who brings the food predicts the arrival of the meat much better. There is an important exception to this rule: taste aversion. A poison causes nausea (US) and subsequent taste aversion (UR). When food taste (here the CS) is associated with nausea, taste aversion as CR develops even if the delay between CS and US – taste and nausea – is up to 24 hours, as we shall discuss later.

Other timings also lead to weakened conditioning. One example is simultaneous presentation of CS and US; that is, when the bell rings at the same time the meat is delivered. Finally, when the bell rings after the meat is given, the dog presumably enjoys the meat and does not attend to the bell-ringing. The best outcome of classical conditioning has been observed when the CS predicts the US.

To sum up, after repeated CS-US pairings, the CS alone will elicit the CR. The effect of classical conditioning is greatest when the US immediately follows the CS, with the exception of taste aversion.

However, when the dog repeatedly does not get food after it hears the bell, salivation will decrease and finally disappear. This process is called *extinction*. In general terms, when the CS is repeatedly presented without the US, the association between CS and US will weaken, and the CR will decrease in intensity and finally disappear.

Note that extinction does not mean forgetting. After complete extinction, the dog will no longer salivate after the sound of the bell; that is, there will be no CR after presentation of the CS. Yet when the experiment is interrupted and resumed the next day, the ringing of the bell (CS) elicits salivation (CR), but salivation will be less intense. Although US and CS had never been paired after complete extinction, there was a response again. This mechanism is called *spontaneous recovery*, and it means that the dog cannot have forgotten the link between bell-ringing (CS) and food (US). Moreover, an animal can more easily learn a once acquired CS-US association after complete extinction. This rapid reacquisition further bolsters the notion that extinction is not forgetting.

Extinction can also be observed in humans. When Liza encounters dogs that do not bark, she may no longer show a fear response at the sight of a dog. However, when she then encounters one dog that barks, she may rapidly reacquire the conditioned fear response at the sight of a dog.

Two other mechanisms within classical conditioning are generalization and discrimination. Let us assume that a dog was presented with a tone of 800 Hz immediately before it received food. What happens if a tone of 600 Hz is played alone? The dog will salivate but less intensely than with the 800 Hz tone. Actually, the salivation response will decrease in proportion to the distance of the tone to the original tone. When food is paired with an 800 Hz tone, the dog will salivate less when a 600 Hz tone is played and even less when a 400 Hz tone is played. This learning mechanism is called *generalization*. The CR not only appears when the CS is identical to the one presented in the acquisition phase but also when the CS is similar.

When a dog repeatedly receives food after the 800 Hz tone but a weak yet painful electric shock to its paw after the 400 Hz tone, it will salivate after the 800 Hz tone but show a fear response after the 400 Hz tone. This learning mechanism is called *discrimination* because the dog learns to discriminate between the responses to the two tones.

Again, these principles can be translated to human behavior. Liza may have learned her fear from the encounter with a shepherd dog. However, she presumably generalizes the fear response to other dog breeds as well; the more similar a dog is to the one that originally aroused her fear, the more likely she will respond with fear. If her fear stems from encounters with a barking shepherd dog, but she regularly plays with the neighbor's nice golden retriever, she may show a fear of shepherd dogs but not of golden retrievers – a case of discrimination.

Pavlov thought that he had found a general learning principle according to which any CS immediately followed by a US will lead to a CR. This is not quite true. We mentioned earlier the exception of taste aversion, which can be conditioned if nausea follows hours after food intake. In addition, food aversion in rats can be conditioned by pairing food with a poison that causes nausea but much less by pairing food with a shock (Garcia & Koelling, 1966). You may object that nausea is just a more potent US than the pain induced by shock. However, this is not the case. The same authors found that avoidance of an audiovisual stimulus (a light and a sound) was more pronounced if paired with shock than with nausea.

Such observations suggest that conditioning is not a general learning principle but depends on *biological preparedness*. In the study by Garcia and Koelling, organisms pair taste with nausea but not with pain, and they pair audiovisual stimuli with pain but not with nausea. In a demonstration of biological preparedness for humans, Hugdahl and Öhman (1977) conditioned fear by associating pictures with mild but uncomfortable electric shocks. These pictures depicted potentially dangerous objects that are either biologically relevant (snakes, mushrooms) or biologically irrelevant (electric equipment, loose electric cables). Later, the researchers tried to remove these associations by showing the pictures without providing electric shocks, which is the process of extinction. They also instructed participants that from now on, no shock will follow. Supporting the biological preparedness hypothesis, fear from loose electric cables and other human-made artifacts disappeared completely after the instruction, whereas fear from biologically relevant stimuli persisted.

An observation from clinical practice supports biological preparedness for taste aversion in humans. Cancer patients who undergo chemotherapy that produces nausea develop taste aversion to food.

So strong is this association that knowledge about the underlying sources does not help; although patients know that their nausea is caused by chemotherapy and not by the food they have eaten, they retain the taste aversion (Bernstein & Webster, 1980).

A classical study – nowadays deemed unethical – showed that the principles of classical conditioning can explain the emergence of fear in humans (Watson & Rayner, 1920). The two authors tested an infant now known as Little Albert. The boy was frightened of loud noises but not of a white rat or any other animals or objects. Watson and Rayner exposed Albert to the rat (CS), immediately followed by the loud noise from striking a hammer on a suspended steel bar (US). After some pairings of rat and noise, Albert became frightened at the sight of the rat. Watson and Rayner could also show that the fear generalized to white rabbits and even to fur coats but not to toy blocks. That is, fear generalized to similar objects only. The researchers planned to remove the fear using extinction, but Albert moved with his mother before the extinction sessions started. His identity is uncertain to this day, so it never became clear whether he went on to fear furred animals.

Box 1.1 Research ethics

Studies like the ones by Watson and Rayner on Little Albert or by Milgram (1963) on obedience (see Chapter 7) have raised questions about the ethics of conducting research in psychology. The principal objective of research ethics is to preserve the rights and integrity of participants. There are guidelines for conducting psychological research with human participants, the most prominent being those of the American Psychological Association (APA). Let us discuss four important ethical issues.

The first is minimizing harm. Participants in psychological experiments should not undergo treatment that is known to be harmful, like the conditioning of fear in a child.

Second, individuals have to give informed consent to participate in a study. When a participant comes to an experiment, the experimenter has to provide the participant with information about the purpose of the study; complete information on what the participant has to do or to undergo, such as filling out questionnaires or getting injections; potential advantages and disadvantages in participating in the study; what the task will be; and how long the study will take. Participation in psychological studies is voluntary; the participant can withdraw from a study at any time without giving a reason and without having to fear disadvantages. If the participant is a child, both the child (if able to do so) and the child's parents have to provide informed consent.

Third, debriefing after the study provides the participant with all information about the hypotheses of the study. If the study included deception, this information must be disclosed at the end of the experiment. An example of deception is telling a participant that a medication has a sedative effect when its factual effect is arousing. Interestingly, psychologists consider deception to be ethical, whereas behavioral economists do not (see Hertwig & Ortmann, 2001).

The final point pertains to privacy. Data of study participants have to remain anonymous. Data collection is often anonymous, which avoids any problems with this point. However, if a researcher collects data at several time points, the identity of participants must be stored in order to assign the data at different time points to the right person. In this case, the researcher has to use a code for each person. The researcher creates two files: one with the names and codes and one with the codes and data. It is imperative to store the two files in two separate, secure places; only the researcher has access to the identity of the participants. Each researcher must follow these rules of ethical conduct.

The analogy of Little Albert's fear of furred animals to Liza's fear of dogs is obvious. As already noted, seeing a dog has become a CS for Liza because it was associated with the US (barking) that led to the UR (fear). The irony of fear is that people often do not expose themselves to its source; fear may therefore persist and lead to phobias (see Chapter 8). If Liza avoids dogs, she will not have the opportunity to experience that dogs in general are nice; there is therefore no extinction of the fear response. One popular way to stop fear of dogs is thus to expose people to dogs, as we shall discuss in Chapter 8.

Let us look at a slightly different example, where Liza touched a dog and the dog bites her so that she does not touch dogs again. This kind of learning from consequences of one's own behavior is based on principles of operant conditioning.

THE SKINNER BOX: OPERANT CONDITIONING

In classical conditioning people learn an association between two stimuli, the CS and the US. However, when Liza does not touch dogs because she once wanted to pet one and got bitten, her behavior cannot be explained by the principles of classical conditioning; it is difficult to see what the US and the CS should be. Similarly, the young smoker's aggressive behavior at the subway station is hard to explain by classical conditioning. Common sense assumes that aggression may be driven by positive consequences, such as the pleasure to be dominant, or by lack of negative consequences, that is, lack of punishment. Another type of conditioning – *operant conditioning* (sometimes called *instrumental conditioning*) – may be better suited to explain aggressive behavior because it includes learning an association between a behavioral response and its consequences.

Just as Pavlov's dog has been the most prominent paradigm in classical conditioning, the *operant conditioning chamber* (often called the *Skinner box*) has become the distinctive experimental setup for operant conditioning in animals – in B.F. Skinner's studies, most often pigeons or rats. Psychologists before Skinner used cages, boxes, or mazes with a starting point and the goal where food was placed, but these setups required the researcher to lift the animal after every trial back to the cage or to the starting point in the maze. The operant conditioning chamber allows to leave the animal alone and to register multiple responses. It is a cage that consists of a lever and a dispenser for food pellets. Upon pressing the lever, the animal immediately receives a food pellet. A recorder registers each lever press. Usually, it takes some time until the rat or pigeon presses the lever for the first time and gets food. The times for the subsequent lever presses become increasingly shorter.

Edward Thorndike (1898) observed a similar result in his puzzle box experiment to examine the law of effect. A cat sat in the puzzle box and could escape through a door by giving a response, such as pulling a rope or pressing a lever, and sometimes two or more responses combined. Cats needed a long time to escape the first time, but the times became increasingly shorter with the number of trials.

Based on his learning experiments, Thorndike (1898; see Mazur, 2016) formulated the *law of effect*, which states that when a response in a situation is followed by satisfaction, the response is more likely to reoccur; when the response is followed by discomfort, the response is less likely to reoccur. Thorndike was aware that he had to define satisfaction and discomfort in a way that does not depend on the observed situation but that it had to be observed independently. By satisfaction (or "a satisfying state of affairs," as he called it), he meant a state which the animal does nothing to avoid or even tries to preserve. By discomfort, he meant a state which the animal commonly avoids.

Derived from the law of effect, behaviorists claimed that in operant conditioning, a behavioral response is more likely to be repeated when it has positive consequences and less likely to be repeated when it has negative consequences.

Behaviorists distinguished four types of relationship between behavior and consequences: positive reinforcement, negative reinforcement, punishment, and omission. In *positive reinforcement*, a positive event follows a behavioral response; in common parlance, this is a reward. For example, a rat gets food after a lever press, or a boy gets praise after cleaning up his room. The positive event strengthens the response, which means that the rat or the child is more likely to show the same response again. In *negative reinforcement*, a behavioral response removes an unpleasant stimulus; for example, an animal can escape an ongoing electric shock to the foot by jumping into another compartment of the cage. Both positive and negative reinforcement *increase* the probability of the behavioral response. *Punishment* means that an unpleasant stimulus follows the behavioral response; for example, a rat receives an electric shock upon entering a chamber in a maze, or a child receives a rebuke upon misbehaving. As a consequence, the rat or child is less likely to show the same response again. Finally, in *omission* (sometimes called "negative punishment"), a behavioral response removes a pleasant state. For example, a boy gets his favorite breakfast cereal each morning but does not get it after he oversleeps. Both punishment and omission *decrease* the probability of the behavioral response.

Sometimes, positive and negative reinforcement work in unison to create a vicious circle. One instance is a father waiting with his daughter at a supermarket checkout. Just before the checkout, there is a display of all kinds of candies. The daughter begins to beg that she wants to get a candy, then she whimpers, and at the end she screams. At first the father resists, but when the screaming becomes too tiring and embarrassing, he finally gives in. At this moment, both his and the daughter's behavior are reinforced. For the child, the candy is a positive reinforcement for screaming, increasing the probability of her behavioral response; next time at the checkout, the daughter is likely to scream again. For the father, giving in and buying the candy leads to negative reinforcement because it ends the unpleasant screaming, increasing the frequency of his behavioral response; next time, he is likely to give in again. As the behaviors of both father and child are mutually reinforced, their frequencies increase. The child will leave out begging and whimpering and begin screaming at once; the father will also shorten the duration of getting tired and embarrassed and give in earlier. Seemingly complex behavior like vicious circles of reinforcement can be explained by simple laws of operant conditioning.

Another phenomenon explained by operant conditioning is *learned helplessness* (Maier & Seligman, 1976). We have seen that animals learn to escape a shock by jumping to another compartment of the cage, resulting in negative reinforcement. However, what happens when animals are given shocks without the possibility to escape? In studies on learned helplessness, dogs that could not escape shocks in a first session did not escape shocks in later sessions. They just remained seated in the cage even though they would have had the opportunity to escape. Later, learned helplessness served as a model for depression and for the passivity of underachievers at school. If humans are criticized on whatever they do, they become passive and miss opportunities to act where they could make a change. When George prepares for tests and nevertheless gets bad grades, he probably will stop preparing for tests because his behavior does not get reinforced.

When introducing positive reinforcement, we have considered the case where a rat received reinforcement after every lever press, which is called *continuous reinforcement*. What happens when reinforcement is not given after every behavioral response? In this case, we might expect that the frequency of the behavioral response decreases because it is less likely to be followed by positive reinforcement. However, this is not what happens. After a rat has been trained that a food pellet arrives after each lever press, the experimenter can deliver food only after every 3, and later every 10 or even every 100 lever presses. However, instead of decreasing the frequency of lever presses, such a schedule of reinforcement in fact increases the frequency of the behavioral response – at least until the food pellet is given. After a short pause, the rat begins to respond at a high rate again.

Ferster and Skinner (1957) distinguished four main schedules of reinforcement. A rat that gets food after, say, every 3, 10, or 100 lever presses is on a *fixed ratio* schedule. An example of a person who is rewarded by a fixed ratio schedule is a car dealer who is paid commission after every 10 car sales.

The *variable ratio* schedule would reinforce at a certain rate, for example after every 10 behavioral responses, *on average*; the reinforcement could be delivered after 2 or 11 or 17 responses. This schedule is especially suited to elicit a high response rate. It is no coincidence that the chances of winning in gambling follow variable ratio schedules. If a slot machine would yield gains in accordance with a fixed ratio schedule, a player would wait for the gain and then stop. The very unpredictability of variable ratio schedules keeps gamblers inserting coin after coin into the slot machine.

Two other schedules yield reinforcement after a certain interval instead of a certain number of responses. In the *fixed interval* schedule, reinforcement is provided at regular intervals. For example, a rat gets a food pellet on the first lever press after 2 minutes, regardless of the number of lever presses up to then. This schedule leads to a low rate of behavioral responses at the beginning of the interval and an increasing rate towards the end of the interval. Let us assume that you play tennis at the world-class level, and every Monday the ATP (Association of Tennis Professionals) rankings appear. You will rarely check the rankings during the week, but as the time of their publication approaches, you may look up the site more and more frequently until the rankings are online. The reinforcement consists of finally seeing the ranking. A *variable interval* schedule provides reinforcement after a certain interval, for example every 5 minutes, *on average*; the reinforcement could be given after 1, 6, or 8 minutes. This schedule supports a steady rate of responses. An example of a variable ratio schedule in the human domain is a girl who helps her grandparents with gardening and receives $5 every now and then but not at a regular interval.

Operant conditioning has become important in behavior analysis and behavior modification. We explored earlier the vicious circle that developed when the father reinforced the daughter's screaming by buying a candy, and the daughter reinforced her father's behavior when she stopped screaming. To examine such patterns of reinforcement is the task of behavior analysis. Once psychologists know what kind of reinforcements are at work, they can begin to change them. Such behavior modification is at the heart of behavior therapy (see Chapter 8).

Together the theories of classical and operant conditioning provide powerful explanations for the emergence of behavior. Behaviorism built on a philosophical tradition called *empiricism*, which claimed that humans are born with some basic reflexes but otherwise the mind at birth is a blank slate. Humans have to learn everything from scratch; the environment determines what people learn and how they behave. There is no inherited or inborn knowledge, preferences, or instincts, and if there were talents or abilities, their role would be much smaller than the role of learning. In the nature-nurture debate, the behaviorists claim that nurture plays the major role. John Watson, who performed the Little Albert experiment and is one of the founding fathers of behaviorism, echoed this tradition when he claimed,

> Give me a dozen healthy infants, well-formed, and my own specified world to bring them up in and I'll guarantee you to take any one of them at random and train him to become any type of specialist I might select – doctor, lawyer, artist, merchant-chief, and, yes, even beggar-man and thief, regardless of his talents, penchants, tendencies, abilities, vocations, and race of his ancestors.
>
> (Watson, 1945/1924, p. 82)

According to behaviorists, being aggressive, fearing dogs, or having learning difficulties all depend on an individual's learning history that can be explained in terms of classical or operant conditioning. However, some observations challenged this assumption.

DIFFICULTIES WITH BEHAVIORISM

The philosopher Thomas Kuhn (1962) noted that scientific progress happens linearly as long as new evidence does not contradict the crucial assumptions of the reigning theoretical framework (or "paradigm," as Kuhn called it). Most often, difficulties emerge in the form of observations that cannot be explained within the traditional theories. At first, scientists treat these difficulties as anomalies and try to add new theoretical assumptions that help explain the observations within the traditional paradigm. Only if the difficulties become so overwhelming that there is no way to explain new observations within the old paradigm is the time ripe for a new paradigm that replaces the old one. This radical transition from one paradigm to another often happens within a short time; that is why Kuhn called these sudden changes "scientific revolutions." In this section I review the difficulties with behaviorism. The next chapter discusses the "cognitive revolution" that superseded behaviorism as the reigning paradigm in psychology.

To undermine the crucial assumptions of behaviorism, one would have to show that there is learning that cannot be explained in terms of classical or operant conditioning.

A first observation that cannot be explained within the behaviorist paradigm is learning in the absence of reward, reported by Edward Tolman (1948). For this demonstration, a rat is placed in a maze with several arms. Usually, there is food in a goal box at the end of one arm but not in the others. In line with the laws of operant conditioning, rats explore the maze and are reinforced with food when they reach the end of the correct arm, which increases the probability that the rat enters the same arm on the next trial; the rats learn where the food is located within the maze. A control group did not get food and therefore made more errors until it reached the goal box. Tolman added a third group of rats that freely explored the maze for 10 trials without food reward before food was introduced in the 11th trial. If the learning depended on reinforcement, no more learning would have been observed in this group than in the control group of rats that never received the food reward, and considerably less learning than the group of rats that had gotten the food reward from the first trial on. According to the laws of operant conditioning, learning in Tolman's study is a consequence of reinforcement; there should be no learning without reward.

Tolman's finding contradicted the principles of operant conditioning. During the first 10 trials, rats that received a food reward after the 10th trial did not differ in their responses from the control group that did not receive a food reward. This effect could be expected because the two groups had the same treatment during the first 10 trials. However, after the rats got the reward once in the 11th trial, they were as good at finding the food as the group of rats that had gotten the reward from the beginning and better than the rats that never had gotten a reward. In other words, the rats in Tolman's experiment learned about the maze even if they were not rewarded. This phenomenon is called *latent learning*. It needs more than the law of effect and the principles of reinforcement to explain this observation. Tolman (1948) concluded from this and other experiments that free exploration was sufficient for rats to learn the spatial arrangement of the maze; they acquire, as he called it, a *cognitive map*, or a representation of the environment in memory. More recent research discovered the biological basis of cognitive maps and their acquisition through exploration (see Moser, Moser, & McNaughton, 2017).

Second, people learn from observation, a finding that is difficult to explain in terms of operant conditioning. In a now classical study, Albert Bandura (1965) showed nursery school children a television clip of an adult person who behaved aggressively against a Bobo doll. In the clip, the adult punched the doll on the nose or pummeled it on the head with a mallet and made aggressive remarks. The adult role model was either rewarded or punished for hitting the Bobo doll. Then the experimenter let the child play alone with various toys, including a Bobo doll, balls, and a mallet. When children observed that the adult role model had been rewarded by being given candies and soft drinks, they behaved more aggressively against the Bobo doll than children who observed an adult role model that was punished by being reprimanded. The children seemed to learn that they will not be punished for aggression against the doll when the role model was rewarded, and that there will be punishment in the form of reprimands when the role model was rebuked. In other words, there was no need for direct reward or punishment of aggressive behavior in children, as in operant conditioning. In addition, Bandura tested a third group of children who viewed an aggressive role model who was neither rewarded nor punished. Interestingly, children in this group behaved like children who observed a role model that was rewarded for being aggressive. The lack of consequences of the model's aggressive behavior encouraged aggressive behavior in children.

This experiment not only extended learning theory but also falsified (that is, proved wrong) a prominent theory to alleviate violence and aggression. The Greek philosopher Aristotle entertained the idea that aggression could be stopped by letting people watch violence. This mechanism of "letting off steam" was called *catharsis*. Sigmund Freud later built this idea into his theory. Simply put, people can replace real aggression by watching aggression. Observation of aggression is supposed to have the same effect as real aggression but is less harmful for society. The idea is elegant, but Bandura's study proves it wrong. Indeed, large-scale studies and historical data on watching aggression suggest that catharsis does not work. The watching of aggression by children and adolescents may even increase later expression of aggression, which contradicts the idea that people can let off steam and become less aggressive by watching boxing or wrestling.

Taken together, the studies on maze learning without reinforcement and observation learning suggest that principles of conditioning are not sufficient to explain behavior. People do not simply react to their environment, but they act according to how they interpret a situation. Terms like *cognitive map, memory*, and *observation* belong to the realm of cognitive psychology.

Recommended literature

Overview

Mazur, J.E. (2016; see references).

Two classical primary sources discussed in the last section

Bandura, A. (1965; see references).
Tolman, E.C. (1948; see references).

FILLING THE BLACK BOX

Cognitive psychology

After high school, Adrian decided to become an architect. He might have thought that the risk of unemployment is low and the prospect of earning a good salary is high. This kind of thinking is called *utilitarian* and is the hallmark of *rational decision-making*. People weigh the advantages and disadvantages of an action and decide on the basis of *maximized expected utility*, which is the best outcome they could expect. There are two factors that determine expected utility of an action: the probability that an outcome obtains and the value of the outcome. An action has high expected utility when the probability of the most valued outcome is high. For Adrian, becoming an architect would have high expected utility if he thinks it is probable that he passes all exams and becomes an architect, and if he values the consequences of being an architect, such as earning much or enjoying the work. This kind of rationality has been called means-ends rationality because decision makers look at means to optimize ends. The theory assumes that people have complete information and use it when they determine expected utility.

In traditional economics, humans are seen as rational decision makers who calculate maximized expected utility to decide their course of action. Humans are seen as *maximizers*. We shall see towards the end of the chapter that people do not always act in accordance to means-ends rationality but use heuristics – rules of thumb that lead to good enough outcomes but save time. In this view, humans are *satisficers* who are content with the first outcome that they consider satisfactory.

Regardless of whether humans calculate expected utility or use heuristics, they are thinking about their behavior, and their thoughts guide their actions. As the term "thinking" was part of the black box in behaviorism and hence did not exist in the vocabulary of the behaviorists, a new kind of psychology had emerged, cognitive psychology. This new psychology deals with the mental processes between the occurrence of a stimulus and a behavioral response.

In Figure 2.1, the elements above the dashed line belong to the observable behavior explored by the behaviorists. The elements below the line are mental processes that behaviorists claimed to belong to the black box. Cognitive psychologists assumed that a stimulus is perceived and then encoded; that is, the perceived input has to be categorized and interpreted in order to be ready for storage in memory. Later, information stored in memory is retrieved in order to prepare inferences, judgments, and decisions that precede the behavioral response. For example, if Anne goes to an exhibition of local animals where there is a snake, she first perceives the stimulus and then classifies it as a member of the category *snakes*. Information about the snake – its shape, color, movements – is then stored in memory. She also stores what she reads about the snake; for example, that it is poisonous. When Anne later encounters a snake

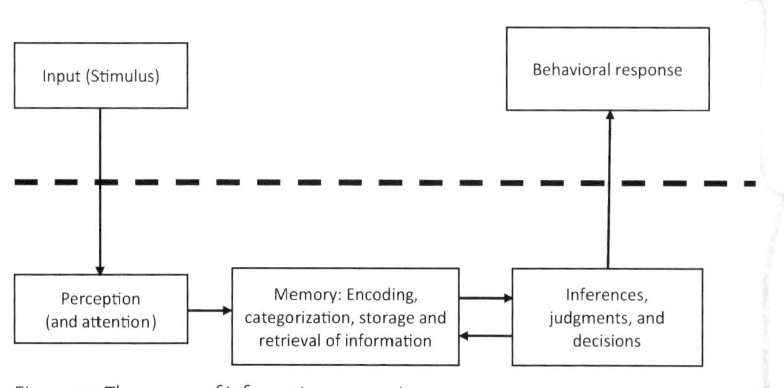

Figure 2.1 The course of information processing
Source: Simplified and adapted from Greifeneder, Bless, & Fiedler, (2018).

during a hike through the wilderness, she perceives it and retrieves information from her memory. As the snake looks similar, she concludes that it could be poisonous. She infers that the snake might be dangerous and decides not to approach it. Note that Anne does not act according to whether the snake really is poisonous but according to her belief that it could be poisonous. According to cognitive psychologists, it is not the objective environment that determines behavior – as behaviorists claimed – but the environment as interpreted by the person.

Cognition denotes the encoding, storage, manipulation, and retrieval of information. Cognition includes mental capacities like perception, categorization, memory, thought, language, judgment, and decision-making. Remember that behaviorists wanted to limit psychology to the study of behavior because they thought that cognition cannot be studied scientifically. However, with the advent of computers in the 1950s, rigorous study of cognitive processes became possible; the cognitive revolution took off.

To this purpose, psychologists assumed that the human brain is a kind of computer and cognitive processes are programs. The brain is the hardware and the mind the software. Psychologists cannot directly observe cognitive processes, but they can manipulate the input in a way that the output becomes informative. For example, when children make mistakes in solving addition tasks, such as 27 + 29 = 46, researchers can analyze what could have gone wrong with the "program." In this case, learners have not considered that they have to add 10 because the addition of the rightmost digits, 7 + 9, yields 16. Further tasks, for example 38 + 24, could confirm the process underlying the mistake if the child answers 52, and teachers can directly address the error in the "program" and teach the child how to correctly compute additions with carrying.

When seen as a computer, the human mind has a general architecture with one common programming language. The notion of *modularity of the mind* (Fodor, 1983) assumes specialized modules, such as vision, hearing, or language, and a central processing system that functions like a computer. The specialized modules, often at the periphery of the mind, process only certain types of information, such as light, sound, or speech; they are *domain specific*. Information coming from the specialized modules is translated into the language of the central system that classifies, changes, stores, and retrieves information. This central system is *domain general*, which means that the same format of knowledge structures or "mental language" is used for navigating through a house, remembering where we last found food, learning mathematics, finding a mate, and detecting whether another person wants to cheat us. Fodor also claimed that the central system hardly influences the highly specialized and fast peripheral modules.

Other psychologists postulated that it is more plausible to see the human mind as a set of modules that functions like a Swiss Army knife with its different blades that all have a specific function. Each module serves a specific ability, such as navigating, foraging, dealing with numbers, mating, and for detecting cheating. In this view, cognition is domain specific. In contrast to Fodor's view, not only the peripheral sensory systems and language are organized as independent modules but also thought and reasoning. However, classical cognitive psychology is still inspired by Fodor's notion of modularity that distinguishes peripheral modules for perception and a central system to process and interpret information in a unitary format.

PERCEPTION AND ATTENTION

The acquisition of information starts with perception of objects from the environment. *Attention* is the process by which our goals, interests, or salient features of the environment direct perception to particular objects. We first discuss perception and then attention.

Perception

First the person perceives a stimulus. The limit at which a human can perceive an object is the *absolute threshold*. Human perceptual capacities are miraculous. A person may see a candle burning at a distance of 30 miles (around 50 kilometers) on a dark, clear night without other sources of light or hear a clock tick at 20 feet (6 meters) under otherwise quiet conditions.

Traditionally, perception has been considered an all-or-nothing event – either you see it or you do not. The absolute threshold is in this tradition. By contrast, *signal detection theory* considers perception of an object as a *judgment*, that is, an inference derived from the evidence at hand and own knowledge (see Box 2.1).

Box 2.1 Signal detection theory

Imagine you walk in the grass and you suddenly notice an elongated shape in front of you. You first think it is a snake but then you see it is a stick. This was a false alarm. When we disentangle this situation systematically, there are four possibilities (Table 2.1). A signal – in this case the snake – may be present or absent. The perceiver may judge that yes, it is a snake or no, it is not. The combination of the signal and the judgment yields four cells. If the signal is present and the judgment is yes, it is a *hit*. This is the case when there is a snake and you judge it to be a snake. In our example, the snake was absent (it was a stick instead) but you judged it to be a snake – a *false alarm*. In the case of the snake, a false alarm may be not as bad as a *miss* – which means there is a snake but you think there is none. Finally, when the signal is absent and you judge it to be absent, it is a *correct rejection*.

The signal detection theory can be applied broadly. We shall discuss in Chapter 8 cases of overdiagnosis where it might be better to have misses.

Table 2.1 The four cells of signal detection theory

		Signal (Snake)	
		Present	Absent
Judgment ("Snake")	Yes	Hit	False Alarm
	No	Miss	Correct Rejection

Psychologists have assumed that when we see a stimulus, for example a snake, we perceive first parts of it – the elongated body, the head, its movements – and then infer from these partial impressions that this must be a snake. This kind of perception includes ***bottom-up processing*** because we see first the parts and infer the whole. There is another possibility, though. If someone tells us that there are many snakes in a region, we expect to see it and just have to confirm it. This way of perceiving the snake includes ***top-down processing*** because it proceeds from the whole to its parts. However, most experts in the field assume that perception is always bottom up; expectations do not change what we see (see Firestone & Scholl, 2016). Figure 2.1 at the beginning of this chapter depicts this notion by showing an arrow from perception to memory (bottom up; in the graph from left to right) but not from memory to perception (top down).

This idea fits Fodor's notion of modularity of the mind discussed earlier. According to the modularity idea, specialized perceptual modules take in information and translate it to the computational language of the central system; however, the central system cannot influence the peripheral system. Top-down processes may change how we direct our attention and what we infer from what we see or hear. For example, we may watch out for snakes and infer that some elongated shape or hissing sound stems from a snake. This is top-down processing because attention and thought are guided by our expectations. However, the images we see or the sounds we hear do not change due to our expectations.

We not only perceive objects but also other people, especially their faces. Face perception is special. There are three kinds of evidence: cognitive, clinical, and neuroscientific. In a now classical cognitive experiment, Tanaka and Farah (1993) compared face perception with object perception. When you have seen a photograph of the face of Larry and afterwards you see a nose in isolation, you will have difficulty deciding whether it is Larry's or not. You will be much better able to correctly recognize Larry's nose when it is placed on his face. This observation shows that people process faces as a whole. By contrast, if you see a house and afterwards a window in isolation, you are about as able to decide whether the window belongs to the house as when you have to recognize the window within the whole house. Faces are special because they are processed as a whole, whereas objects are to a higher degree processed in parts.

Clinical evidence for the special status of face comes from "face blindness," or *prosopagnosia*. People who suffer from that disorder cannot recognize faces. In everyday life, these people may function quite well because they use non-facial cues to recognize another person, such as one's voice or clothes. The disorder is limited to *human* faces. This fact is illustrated by a man who suffered from prosopagnosia as a consequence of several strokes. He decided to change careers and began to raise sheep. Although he was unable to recognize the faces of his relatives, he was perfectly able to distinguish the faces of his sheep (McNeil & Warrington, 1993).

Finally, brain imaging studies showed that the fusiform area, a part of the human visual system, is specialized for face perception. This area is activated when faces are presented but not when objects or hands are shown (Kanwisher, McDermott, & Chun, 1997). To summarize, there is ample evidence for the assumption that face processing is special and different from the perception of objects or other body parts.

Attention

When we perceive the environment, we often focus our attention on one object and neglect others. Attention has often been construed as a filter that selects information. For example, when you talk to a friend at a party, you try to exclude all distracting sounds in order to understand what your friend says. It looks like you do not process the speech around you and select early on the information you wish to process. These assumptions are made by *early selection models* of attention. However, one observation led scientists to doubt that early selection models are accurate. You may have experienced a situation where you talked to a friend and ignored everything around you – but suddenly, you heard your name. This observation has been called the *cocktail party effect*. How would it be possible to hear your name if you filtered out all utterances that do not stem from your friend? Therefore, *late selection models* of attention claimed that the mind analyzes all incoming information and then filters out the irrelevant pieces of information. Several models have been proposed since, such as attenuation instead of filtering out of incoming information, movable filters that allow more flexible selection of information, or attention as a process with limited capacity that requires effort. Whatever the right theory turns out to be, it will neither be a pure early selection model nor a pure late selection model.

A famous empirical demonstration, the *Stroop effect*, shows that we cannot filter out all information. In the first trial, the experimenter presents a page with 20 blue, red, green, and yellow rectangles. Participants have to name the correct color as fast as possible. In the second trial, participants are shown the color words "BLUE," "RED," "GREEN," and "YELLOW." Crucially, the 20 color words are written in an ink that does not match their meaning. "BLUE" is written in red, "YELLOW" in green, "RED" in yellow, and so on. Participants have to name the ink in which the word is written. When the word "BLUE" appears in red ink, they have to say "red." It turns out that naming the color of words written in the wrong ink takes more time than to name the color of the rectangles. As reading is an overlearned practice, it is not possible to filter out the meaning of the color word in the non-matching ink. When you see the red word "BLUE," you automatically read it, which leads to interference with the naming task. Most people cannot control their attention to a degree that they can suppress automatic reading of the color words.

Automaticity has become an important topic in the psychology of attention, categorization, learning, thought, judgment, and behavior. Automatic processes are highly efficient: they often happen unintended and cannot be controlled, as we have seen in the Stroop effect; and they are sometimes unconscious, for example in stereotype formation (Devine, 1989; see Chapter 7).

Intentional, controlled, and conscious processes are more precise than automatic processes, but they are slow. This leads to a tradeoff between speed and accuracy. In terms of the distinction made earlier, maximizers can be slow but reach the maximum accuracy possible; satisficers can be fast but just good enough.

MEMORY

From the early 1990s to date, the *Innocence Project* has helped lead to the overturning of more than 300 wrongful convictions in the United States through DNA evidence. In more than 70 percent of these convictions, misidentification by eyewitnesses played a major role (see Wixted & Wells, 2017). What went wrong?

We discussed in the introduction that one of the first studies on memory (Ebbinghaus, 1913/1885) observed that people forget fast. The decline of memory is strongest right after encoding. However, eyewitnesses do not simply forget how the perpetrator looks; their memory often seems to have undergone changes. In this section, we are going to see that memory is not just the reproduction of what has been encoded. When people encode or retrieve information, they try to make sense of it and adapt it in ways that makes it intelligible. Memory is a constructive process, examined in a study by English psychologist Frederic Bartlett (1932). His participants read a short story, the "The War of the Ghosts," and had to reproduce the story at a later time.

"The War of the Ghosts" was a mysterious story about two young men from Egulac who went down the river to hunt seals. A canoe with warriors came and wished to take them along. One of the young men remarked that his relatives did not know where he had gone and went home while the other man went with the warriors. He later thought they were ghosts because they told him that he was hit, but he did not feel sick. The story ends, "When the sun rose he fell down. Something black came out of his mouth. His face became contorted. The people jumped up and cried. He was dead."

When participants reproduced the story, they did not just repeat back what they read earlier; and forgetting did not mean that they just randomly left out some parts of the story. In Bartlett's study, individuals often left out information that they did not understand, such as the ghosts. They changed contents in order to render the story more intelligible, for example, "being hit but not feeling sick" turned into a wound or "something black" turned into blood. Some abstract details transformed into concrete ones; in one of the reproductions, "relatives" became "the old mother."

The idea that remembering is a constructive process has consequences for eyewitness testimony. As long as we think of memory as a store of information that a witness retrieves, eyewitness testimony seems to be a reliable source. However, it turns out that memory of eyewitnesses is malleable and may lead to wrong convictions. How can such mistakes happen?

In a classical demonstration of the malleability of eyewitness memory, participants saw a film clip about a crash involving two cars (see Loftus, 1979). Half of the participants saw that a car stood at a stop sign before the crash, while the other half saw that the car stood at a yield sign. After watching the clip, half of the participants had to answer the question, "Did you see a stop sign?" and the other half had to answer the question, "Did you see a yield sign?" Importantly, half of the participants saw the same sign they were later asked about – either twice *stop* or twice *yield*. For the other half of the participants, the signs shown in the film clip and asked about were different – either *stop* turned to *yield* or *yield* turned to *stop*. Finally, participants had to choose what kind of sign they saw in the film clip: *stop* or *yield*. If people just registered what they saw, the question about the stop sign or the yield sign should not lead to any differences between groups. However, this was not what Loftus found. When the signs seen in the film clip and later asked about were the same, 75 percent of the participants chose the correct sign. Yet, when the signs were different, only 41 percent of the participants chose the correct sign. This experiment provided the first evidence for the *misinformation effect*. A question about a relevant detail asked between seeing a scene and remembering it can mislead a person to retrieve the wrong information.

Witnesses do not only have difficulties identifying details of a scene but also identifying faces (for a recent review, see Wixted & Wells, 2017). Misidentification has been a frequent cause of wrongful convictions. The usual way to identify a perpetrator has been lineups where about six people stand in a row, including the suspect and so-called foils who are not suspects in the crime case. The witness (who is often the victim) is brought in and has to identify the perpetrator or state that the perpetrator is not among the suspects – after all, the police may have caught the wrong suspect.

An intricate issue is the choice of the foils in the row. For example, if five sturdy policemen are in a row with a haggard drug addict suspected of theft, a witness may misidentify the drug addict as the thief at above chance level. One way to circumvent the problem of a witness choosing a suspect simply because he stands out is to ask non-involved individuals to point to the person in the row who is most probably the perpetrator. If these people unrelated to the crime pick the suspect with above chance probability, the lineup seems to be biased, and the police officers have to select new foils. There is evidence that it is better to choose foils that resemble the description of the perpetrator by witnesses than foils that resemble the suspect. If the foils resemble the description, the chances that a witness chooses a foil remain the same. However, when the foils resemble the suspect, the chances decrease that the witness identifies the perpetrator.

Research has also found that identifications brought forward with confidence are more likely to be accurate than identifications after hesitation. It is therefore important not only to register whether the witness picked the suspect but also to record confidence. Importantly, confidence only predicts accuracy when done at the time of identification, not when the witness during the trial weeks later tells with confidence that the suspect is the perpetrator.

To summarize, this section showed that memory is a constructive process in which our thought and judgmental processes play a crucial role in order to make sense of a situation, such as a story or what people have seen as an eyewitness. How we remember depends on how we think.

THOUGHT

Astrology has no scientific basis. However, you may have heard an uncle say at a family reunion that an astrologer gave him his horoscope and he was impressed because it was 100 percent accurate! Why do recipients of horoscopes think they are accurate despite the lack of scientific validity? Let us discuss two of the most important mechanisms behind this credulity, the first one in passing and the second one in more detail because it is relevant for our later discussion of self-fulfilling prophecy.

Perhaps the most important reason for why people believe in astrology lies in the generality of its language: for example, "You have a great deal of unused capacity which you have not turned to your advantage"; "At times you have serious doubts as to whether you have made the right decision or done the right thing"; "Some of your aspirations tend to be pretty unrealistic." If an astrologer told your uncle that she knows his appearance without seeing him and writes down that he has two eyes, a nose, and a mouth, he would shake his head in disbelief. By contrast, when the astrologer tells him about unused capacity, self-doubts, and unrealistic aspirations, he believes that she has uncovered deep secrets because he does not realize that these inner states are like eyes, nose, and mouth shared by all human beings.

The second reason people believe in horoscopes may have to do with hypothesis testing. Before I come back to belief in astrology, let us look at a classical study and its significance for the psychology of thinking.

In 1960, British psychologist Peter Wason demonstrated the *confirmation bias*, which is a tendency to search for information that confirms rather than contradicts a person's assumptions. He conducted a study in which he presented participants with the number sequence 2 4 6 as an instance of the correct sequence. He instructed the participants to find out the correct rule by creating their own sequences of three numbers. Such inference of a general rule from specific instances is called *induction*. After each sequence, the experimenter provided feedback as to whether the participants' sequence is correct or incorrect, and the participants created the next sequence until they thought they knew the rule, at which point they had to report it to the experimenter. Only few participants found the correct rule on the first attempt. Most participants created sequences, such as 8 10 12, 1 3 5, or −6 −4 −2. Every time, the experimenter responded that the sequence is correct. After some such trials, the participants stated that the rule is "numbers increasing by 2." However, the correct rule was "increasing numbers." Apparently, participants assumed from the beginning – when seeing 2 4 6 – that the rule must be "numbers increasing by 2." They then produced sequences that confirmed their hypothesis but rarely produced sequences that contradicted their preconception – they committed the confirmation bias. In order to arrive at the correct rule it would have been necessary to produce sequences that falsify the hypothesis, here "numbers increasing by 2," for example by creating the sequences 6 4 2, 1 2 3, or 5 7 16. Note that the first sequence contradicts the hypothesis but a participant can still believe that the rule is "numbers increasing by 2" because the sequence 6 4 2 also contradicts the correct rule, "increasing numbers." Only the last two sequences (1 2 3 and 5 7 16) require a revision of the hypothesis because they contradict the original hypothesis, "numbers increasing by 2," but are in accordance with the correct rule, "increasing numbers." Participants would have to create several sequences that contradict their hypothesis in order to check whether one of them nevertheless is in accordance with the correct rule. However, many studies after Wason's demonstration of the confirmation bias showed that people tend to search for information that confirms their preconceptions and rarely search for information that falsifies them. The confirmation bias is ubiquitous and plays an important role when we form impressions of other people (see Chapter 7).

We have asked the question why people trust a pseudoscience like astrology and have come up with one reason: that the statements are so general that they apply to all humans. We now can consider another likely reason. When told that they have self-doubts, readers of a horoscope are likely to look for confirming information under the assumption that the statement is true. They search their memory for events in favor of the hypothesis that they have self-doubts and do not try to retrieve disconfirming evidence.

HEURISTICS AND BIASES

In an experiment by Ross and Sicoly (1979), pairs of spouses were asked about their share of the housework as a percent of the total housework. Each spouse answered separately, so that the sum of the estimates should be no more than 100 percent. However, the sum of the answers on average exceeded 100 percent. Why do spouses overestimate the share of their work in the household? At first, motivational explanations come to mind, for example, that each spouse wants to see himself or herself in the best light. However, the biased estimate can be explained by purely cognitive mechanisms. I can more easily remember my housework than the housework done by my wife, which leads to overestimation of my share. I use the ease with which I can retrieve information as a *heuristic*, which is a rule of thumb that people use as a mental shortcut in judgment and decision-making. Heuristics are often used when a person either has little information or is not motivated to think much about a decision. They are fast and usually quite accurate, but they sometimes lead to *bias*, which is a systematic deviation from an accurate estimate. Psychologists have examined many heuristics and documented several judgmental biases (see Tversky & Kahneman, 1974). Let us look at the availability heuristic.

When people rely on their experience of ease to make a judgment, they use the *availability heuristic*. Amos Tversky and Daniel Kahneman (1973) introduced this heuristic with the following experiment. Participants heard a list of the names of 19 famous men and 20 not so famous women, or vice versa. Later, half of the participants had to judge whether there were more women or men on the list, and the other half of the participants had to recall the names. Participants who heard the names of famous men judged that more men were on the list, while participants who heard names of famous women judged that more women were on the list, despite the fact that the list contained always fewer famous names than non-famous names. Moreover, participants also retrieved more famous names than non-famous names. Tversky and Kahneman concluded that the participants used the ease with which they could recall the names to estimate the frequency of men and women on the list. As famous names were easier to recall, participants thought the gender of the famous names was more frequently listed (for further discussion, see Schwarz, 1998).

Heuristics sometimes lead to bias, as the study by Ross and Sicoly (1979) on the overestimation of their share of the housework by married couples has shown. Overestimation of one's own performance or of positive personal outcomes, such as health and success, is a very common judgmental bias.

As we discussed at the beginning of this chapter, theorists assume that people are rational decision makers and have complete information to calculate expected utility. However, the availability heuristic tells us that the available information might not be accurate. Therefore, a decision based on the available information might be wrong or at least imprecise. In such a case, individuals cannot make fully rational decisions. Another criterion for rationality is invariance, which means that when all information is available to make a decision, it should make no difference how the problem is described (see Kahneman, 2011). However, the assumption of invariance turned out to be wrong; violations of invariance lead to the illusion of control and the status quo bias.

In a classical study on the *illusion of control*, office workers had the opportunity to buy lottery tickets for $1. Half of the buyers could choose a lottery ticket from a bunch of tickets, whereas the other half of buyers was handed a ticket by the experimenter. Some days later, the experimenter came back and told participants that other office workers would like to participate in the lottery, but that he or she ran out of lottery tickets. The experimenter then asked the buyers at what price they were willing to sell back their lottery tickets. Buyers who could choose their ticket required $8.67; buyers who were handed out tickets required $1.96 (Langer, 1975). This is an illusion of control because the buyers thought that a ticket was more valuable if they could exert control over the choice of the ticket; this was not the case, given the probabilistic nature of winning. The illusion of control challenged the rationality of human judgment because rational judgments should be invariant. That is, the expected value of winning the lottery is the same and does not depend on whether a person can choose a ticket.

Similarly, the *status quo bias* emerges because people choose from identical options the one that seems to be the default option (or the status quo). A dramatic instance of this bias can be seen in organ donation. In countries where people have to state that they want to be organ donors, less than 30 percent of adults opt in to become donors. In countries where organ donation is the default and people have to opt out, a majority of adults donates their organs, often more than 90 percent of a country's adult population (Johnson & Goldstein, 2003). Again, the status quo bias violates invariance. Opting in or opting out should not affect the decision.

The heuristics and biases tradition in psychology challenged the economic view of people as rational decision makers (see Kahneman, 2011). In fact, individuals often behave in ways that contradict rational decision-making. However, does this make people irrational? In everyday life, many of the heuristics seem to lead to satisfactory solutions most of the time but may lead people astray under exceptional circumstances. Herbert Simon (1990) introduced the term *bounded rationality* to denote the fact that humans do not maximize outcomes (as rational decision theories would advocate) but satisfice; that is, humans are satisfied with a good enough solution.

One example of satisficing can be seen in the decision tree in Figure 2.2. Medical doctors built a model that used 19 predictors to assess whether a patient is at high risk of dying within the first 30 days of a heart attack. The decision tree in Figure 2.2, including

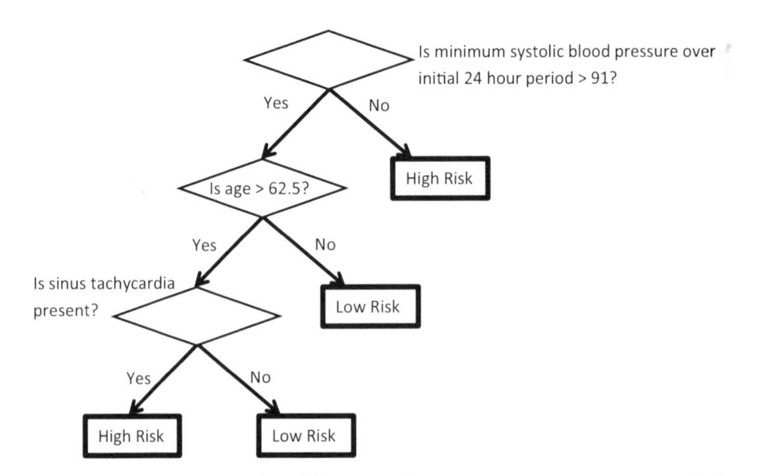

Figure 2.2 Decision tree to classify heart attack patients at emergency units into high-risk and low-risk patients
Source: Adapted from Breiman, Friedman, Olshen, and Stone (1984).

only three decisions, is as good as the complicated model but much faster and easier to apply. Other examples of satisficing are everyday purchase decisions. When people move to a new country and have to find a new brand of toothpaste, they rarely examine all brands on each possible criterion but may simply make sure that it contains fluoride and tastes good. Let us go back to Adrian's decision to become an architect with which we began this chapter. Cognitive theories assume that he weighed the arguments for and against studying architecture, but in thinking about the arguments he might have been prone to bias and overestimated his prospects of success. However, Adrian's decision does not only depend on what he thinks. In everyday life, we often claim that a person chooses an occupation because of his motivation, which is the topic of the next chapter.

Recommended literature

Overview

Reisberg, D. (2012). *Cognition: Exploring the science of the mind*. New York, NY: W.W. Norton.

Classical primary sources

Bartlett, F.C. (1932; see references).
Tversky & Kahneman (1974; see references).

3

WHAT DRIVES BEHAVIOR? MOTIVATION AND EMOTION

When people act, we look for a reason. Why does Joshua try hard at school but George does not? The answer could be motivation that emerges from the desire to satisfy needs. *Motivation* is the driving force that guides behavior; it tells us *why* people behave the way they do. In everyday parlance, the term motivation is often used in a circular way. For example, Joshua's teachers may state that he tries hard because he is motivated by a desire to excel at school. Yet at the same time they may infer that Joshua is motivated by the desire to excel at school because he tries hard. This use of the term *motivation* is circular. When we state that *Behavior A* is caused by a *Motivation B*, we cannot at the same time infer *Motivation B* from *Behavior A*. *Motivation B* has to be observed independently from the consequences it is claimed to engender.

We discuss two main theories of motivation: one based on basic needs and the other on expected utility.

BASIC NEEDS AND MOTIVATION

Early theories of motivation assumed that humans are biologically predisposed to act in a fixed way in certain situations. This is an *instinct* theory of motivation. In the animal kingdom, instincts are common. For example, goslings follow the first moving object they see, which is usually their mother (Lorenz, 1937). Such fixed and automatic responses to a trigger are biologically predetermined and occur in every member of a species; they are not learned and cannot be modified by learning.

In contrast to animal biology, instinct has proven to be a fruitless concept in human psychology. At the beginning, psychologists started with a few basic instincts, such as foraging or mating, but later searched for ever more instincts to explain all human behavior. By 1924, psychologists had proposed more than 14,000 different instincts (see Allport, 1958).

Human behavior is more complex than simple responses to triggers. The purported instincts turned out to have more elaborate underlying mechanisms. Besides, circular definition seemed to be at work in "instinct psychology": when asked why a mother cares for her baby, the answer was maternal instinct. When asked how one knows about maternal instinct, the answer was that we see that the mother cares for her baby. For all these reasons, instincts are no longer used as explanation for human behavior.

Another approach to motivation comes from the idea that humans have needs, such as hunger and thirst. It is essential for survival to satisfy such needs. People have to get energy from food to balance energy expenditure in their daily life. If a person does not eat enough, a drive emerges. A *drive* is an inner tension that motivates an organism to close the gap between the optimal state (sated) and the actual state (hungry) and thus to restore balance. This is the *drive reduction theory* of motivation by Clark Hull (1943). Hull was a behaviorist who combined learning principles with a drive theory. When a rat is hungry, it aims to get food. When the animal in a Skinner box presses the lever and receives food, the positive reinforcement is related to the decrease in tension produced by hunger and therefore in the reduction of the drive. For Hull, positive reinforcement is related to drive reduction, and any behavior that results in drive reduction will therefore be repeated.

However, like instinct theories, drive theories suffered from circular definition as soon as we go beyond undisputed drives like hunger, thirst, and sex. Although the term *drive* is known from Freud's psychoanalysis, it is no longer used in modern scientific theories of motivation. What has survived from drive theories is the concept of need.

Most famous among the need theories is Abraham Maslow's (1943) hierarchy of needs (see Figure 3.1). At the bottom are basic needs like hunger, thirst, and sex. Next follow safety needs, like shelter and protection from pain; love needs, which include family, loving relationships, and friendship; and esteem needs, which are related to achievement and appreciation. At the top of Maslow's pyramid is the need for self-actualization, which includes realization of a person's full potential. Such a person ideally is autonomous, open to new experiences, and thinks independently. Beyond nurturing creativity and high democratic and moral standards, the self-actualized person strives for meaning, inner acceptance, and understanding. Maslow assumed that the lower a need is in the hierarchy, the more basic it is. A higher need can only be addressed when the more basic needs are satisfied. For example, a person is only interested in fulfilling safety needs when she is no longer hungry and thirsty; people who lack shelter and friends do not think about esteem or even self-actualization. Although a plausible assumption, and despite its influence in popular culture, the hierarchy of needs inspired little empirical research, and there is little evidence for Maslow's

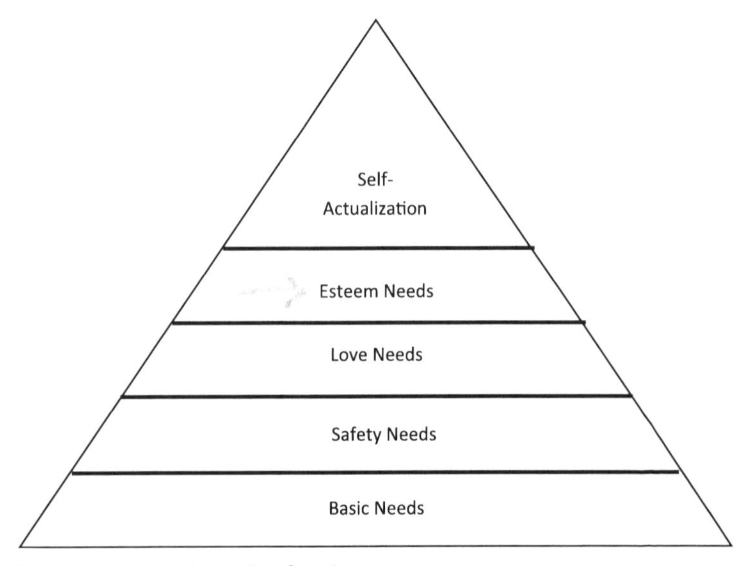

Figure 3.1 Maslow's hierarchy of needs

assumptions. However, the hierarchy of needs led to *self-determination theory* after empirical findings contradicted central assumptions of behaviorism.

Remember the behaviorist tenet that reward increases the probability that a response will be repeated. In 1971, Edward Deci published a study in which students were instructed to solve puzzles during a baseline session, a second session, and a final session. Students in a reward group got money for solving puzzles in the second session but students in a control group did not. Students of both groups did not get a reward for the baseline session and the final session. Deci observed in each session whether students solved puzzles or were distracted by magazines lying on the table. According to behaviorist laws, reinforcement of behavior should increase the frequency of its occurrence. Therefore, students who got a reward for solving puzzles should spend more time solving puzzles in the subsequent final session than in a baseline session prior to the reward session. If, by contrast, behavior is not followed by reinforcement, the frequency of its occurrence decreases, which is the process of extinction. Therefore, the control group should spend less time in the final session than in the baseline session. The actual outcome contradicted this prediction. In the final session, the experimental group actually spent less time on solving puzzles than in the baseline session – despite the reward in between. The control group, by contrast, spent slightly more time on the puzzles in the final session than in the baseline session. This finding undermined the behaviorist notion that reward reinforces a response and hence increases its frequency in subsequent sessions. In fact, money rewards often decrease the interest and engagement in an activity (see Deci, Koestner, & Ryan, 1999).

Such findings show that people are not solely driven by *extrinsic motivation*, which denotes the motivation stemming from sources outside the person. Sources of extrinsic motivation other than monetary reward include praise by others, distinctions, and power. *Intrinsic motivation*, by contrast, relates to an activity done for its own sake, such as a child's play or a hobby.

At the core of *self-determination theory* are three basic, innate needs that support human motivation (see Deci & Ryan, 1985). The first need, *need for autonomy*, means that people want to determine their own actions. Individuals are motivated by knowing that they themselves decide what to do. Second, *need for competence*, which is reminiscent of Maslow's esteem needs, means that people want to show and use their abilities. For example, children are motivated when teachers give them opportunities to practice and demonstrate their abilities. Third, *need for relatedness* means that people want to belong to and be accepted by their family or a group, in line with Maslow's love needs. People are therefore motivated by activities that strengthen the bonds to a group.

Which need is most prevalent may depend on culture. For example, children in Western countries grow up in an *individualistic* culture where they learn that each person is *independent*. By contrast, children in many Asian countries grow up in a *collectivistic* culture, where each person depends on others, or is *interdependent*. Individualism emphasizes personal freedom and individual rights; the emphasis of collectivism lies in duty and obligations for the own community. For Western children, the mother is separate from their independent self; for Asian children, the mother overlaps with their interdependent self. Accordingly, Anglo-American school children are more motivated when they can make a choice themselves than when their mother chooses a task for them. By contrast, Asian American children are more motivated when their mother chooses for them than when they can choose themselves (Iyengar & Lepper, 1999). Apparently, Western children who live in individualistic cultures value the need for competence whereas Asian children who live in collectivistic societies prioritize the need for relatedness.

Self-determination theory has inspired much research. It is highly popular among educators because it promises that they can genuinely motivate students to learn instead of resorting to rewards and force. Another way to look at achievement motivation is through the lens of cognitive theories.

COGNITIVE THEORIES OF MOTIVATION

In the previous chapter, we defined rationality in terms of expected utility, which is the product of value and expected outcomes. When we define outcome in monetary terms, expected utility is a computational affair. For example, when Adrian decides to become an architect, he may multiply the probability that he completes his study by the expected salary. If he does the same for, say, journalist, he may find out the expected utility to become an architect is higher than to become a journalist. In this case, he would prefer becoming an architect because it yields the better financial outcome. This mental computation is a cognitive process.

As the theory of rationality has been developed in economics, one hidden assumption of early expectancy-value theories has been that Adrian is motivated by money; that is, the expected amount of money guides his behavior. However, people are not always motivated by money. Instead of financial prospects, Adrian may compare architecture and journalism on the anticipated enjoyment of the work. That is why psychologists developed expectancy-value theories built on the assumption that humans try to maximize expected utility.

Expectancy-value theories have been extended to achievement motivation in academic contexts and include values like enjoyment or personal importance (see Eccles & Wigfield, 2002). Let us assume that Tina has to choose a course from a course list provided by her high school. *Expectancy-value theories of motivation* assume that Tina's choice depends (1) on expectancy of success and (2) on the value the course has for her (see Figure 3.2).

Expectancy is related to a person's beliefs about (1) whether she is able to execute an action and (2) whether this action results in the desired outcome (Bandura, 1977). The first kind of belief has been called *efficacy belief*. When Tina, a high school student, has to translate a text into French, her belief on whether she will be able to translate the text depends on earlier experience on similar tasks, observing other students, verbal persuasion, and physiological states. Tina thinks that she will be more successful if she has had success in the past, has observed other students solve the same task with success, or when others told her that she can do it. Finally, Tina is more likely to believe that she can translate the text when she is relaxed and less likely to believe in her ability when she is stressed.

The beliefs about whether the behavior results in the desired outcome are *outcome beliefs*. Outcome beliefs are related to *causal attributions*, which are potential explanations of behavior (Weiner, 1979). Such attributions influence her subsequent choices and learning. Let us assume that Tina failed the French language exam. When she thinks that she is unable to learn French, she might decide not to take the French language course again because she will never get a good grade. Ability (or the lack thereof) is a stable cause that cannot

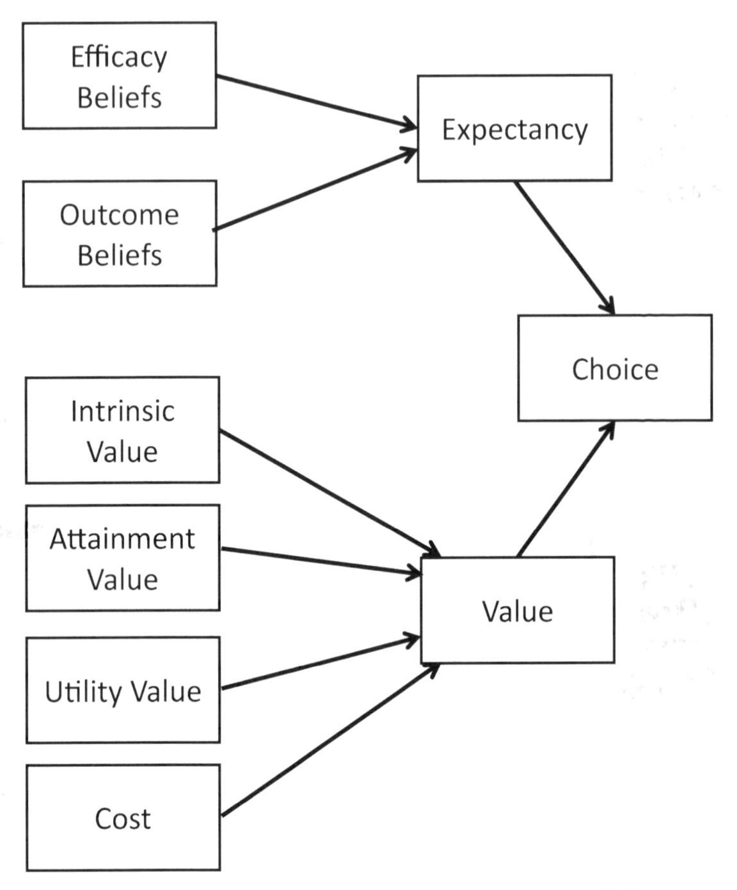

Figure 3.2 Overview on the components of the expectancy-value model of motivation
Source: Simplified after Eccles & Wigfield, (2002).

be changed easily. By contrast, if she thinks that she did not invest enough effort, she is more likely to take the course again and to invest more time for learning. Effort is not a stable cause of success; Tina can increase the likelihood of success by increasing effort.

Taken together, a person might ask why she did not succeed in an exam. Her interpretation of the causes influences whether she will try again or choose other courses. Note that in line with a main tenet of cognitive psychology, expectancy of success is derived from what a person believes and how she interprets the situation, which may or may not accord with the real situation.

Beyond expectancy of success (top part of Figure 3.2), Tina will ask why she should learn French (bottom part of Figure 3.2). Eccles and Wigfield (2002) propose four kinds of values. First, *intrinsic value* refers to how much students enjoy and are interested in an activity, such as learning French. Second, *attainment value* refers to the personal importance of a topic or task. For example, Tina wants to learn French because her grandmother is French Canadian, and speaking French is part of the family identity. Third, *utility value* tells us how helpful a course or a task is in reaching external goals, such as admission to a top university or relevance for a future career. Tina might choose to learn French because it helps her to get an international business degree. Finally, *costs* are negative aspects in an activity, such as effort. Although Tina may think that French is important and useful, she may dread the effort she has to invest in learning the language.

Several interventions have been developed to increase the various facets of value, especially to increase interest in mathematics and science (for a review, see Reber, Canning, & Harackiewicz, 2018). To increase *intrinsic* value, interventions aim at connecting subject matter with a person's existing interests. For example, tasks on probability calculus can be embedded in topics like music, sports, or gaming. The learning materials are then adapted to each individual student, or students can choose a topic in which instruction and tasks on probability calculus are embedded. Such personalization of instruction attracts attention to the learning materials and enhances enjoyment in the task.

To increase *attainment* value, educators can increase identity-based motivation. The basic idea is that students do not classify difficult tasks as "nothing for me" but as something "important for me." This form of using a student's identity led to school-related improvements for disadvantaged minority students (Oyserman, 2015).

Interventions to increase the *utility value* of a subject may help increase both interest and performance. A simple way to increase utility value would be to tell students why the subject is relevant for everyday life or for their future career. For example, as the author of this book, I might tell you that to learn something about expectancy-value theories of motivation helps you understand the motivation underlying career and other choices. This would be a (very brief) utility value intervention. Another way to increase perceived utility value consists in instructing students to write down how the current subject is relevant for their life and future career. Several studies showed that particularly students with low interest or low performance expectations benefit from written utility-value interventions.

Students may enjoy a subject and find it important both personally and for their career, but they eschew the costs. It is of course desirable to get maximal value for minimal cost. Yet sometimes, people have to accept higher costs to get higher returns in terms of value and success. "No pain, no gain," as the folk saying goes. Indeed, there are situations where students learn better from difficult tasks but they underestimate the learning outcome and prefer to learn from easier tasks. By circumventing such "desirable difficulties," they forgo an opportunity for optimal learning (for a summary, see Reber, 2016). We shall see later that self-control and conscientiousness are important predictors of academic and occupational success. People high in these two traits learn more because they persist longer in the face of difficulties; persistence increases the costs but the success outweighs the invested effort.

When we come back to our examples at the beginning of the chapter, we might find out that George is not motivated to learn because he lacks a sense of autonomy or because he thinks that his difficulties stem from lack of ability and that ability cannot be changed by learning. Joshua might try hard to learn because he wants a good job when he is grown up – which adds utility value. As said at the outset, we have to determine the motivation independent of the action – we need to assess the motivation to learn and the act of learning separately. When it comes to Liza making long detours to avoid dogs, what is her motivation? Obviously, she is motivated by fear. As we shall see, emotions include an action tendency and therefore can motivate behavior.

WHAT IS AN EMOTION?

In everyday life, people do not have trouble understanding the statement, "Liza is afraid of dogs." In science, it has been much harder to gain a proper understanding of fear and emotion in general. When Liza encounters a dog, the commonsense assumption is that she runs away from the dog because she feels fear. William James (1884), one of the founding fathers of modern psychology, challenged common sense in a famous paper titled "What Is an Emotion?" In James's view, Liza would not run away from the dog because she feels fear but that she feels fear because she runs away from the dog. Liza (1) sees the dog, (2) runs away, and (3) shows bodily responses like sweating, a racing heart, or a feeling of unease. These latter reactions belong to the viscera, which are the inner organs; with regard to emotions, especially the heart and the intestines. According to James, this bodily reaction *is* fear, and not just an expression of fear. As the same theory was independently and at around the same time developed by the Danish physician Carl Lange, it became known as the *James-Lange theory* of emotion.

Physiologist Walter Cannon (1927) summarized the evidence pertinent to the James-Lange theory and concluded that the data do not support the theory. He listed five pieces of evidence that falsified William James's theory.

First, according to the James-Lange theory, the separation of the brain from the rest of the body disables an animal to show bodily responses that are supposed to constitute the emotion. Such an animal could no longer feel emotions. However, studies with dogs and cats showed that the total separation of viscera from the brain does not result in a marked change in emotional behavior. Later studies have shown that emotions felt by humans suffering from spinal cord injury were of similar intensity as the emotions felt by individuals with intact spinal cord. Second, bodily reactions are supposed to be emotion specific. There should be one bodily state for fear, another for anger, still another for joy, and so on. Yet identical bodily changes occur in very different emotional and non-emotional states. Third, if the viscera caused the feelings, one would expect that the organs that cause the experience, especially the intestines, are very sensitive. However, the viscera are relatively insensitive organs that have only a few nerve receptors and therefore cannot give rise to distinctive feelings. Fourth, emotions are felt immediately but visceral changes are too slow in order to be the cause of our emotional experience.

A final prediction of the James-Lange theory is that an injection of adrenaline, a drug that leads to strong visceral activation, should lead to strong emotion. A study by Marañon (1924) showed that this was not the case. However, he found one exception. When the participants thought of a strongly emotional event, such as the death of a parent or serious illness of a child, they reported feeling an emotion. This observation led to the two-factor theory of emotion and a famous experiment (Schachter & Singer, 1962).

According to the *two-factor theory of emotion*, both physiological arousal and the interpretation of a situation must be present in order to elicit an emotion. Most participants in Marañon's study lacked an explanation for their arousal and therefore did not experience an emotion. However, as soon as arousal can be explained as stemming from a situation that indicates, for example, success or danger, people will feel an emotion. The two-factor theory of emotion predicts that both physiological arousal and cognitive interpretation are necessary for an emotion, but only the two factors combined are sufficient. Physiological arousal is necessary for *that* an emotion is felt; cognitive interpretation is necessary for *what* emotion is felt.

This is indeed what Schachter and Singer (1962) found. They tested these assumptions in an experiment that combined injection with adrenaline and a situation that might trigger emotion. The experimenters created euphoria or anger by having a confederate to the experimenter behave in a way that induced these feelings in the participants. The authors found support for their hypotheses. When a placebo was given no emotion was felt, regardless of the situation; the participants lacked physiological arousal to feel an emotion. By contrast, adrenaline injection led to positive affect when combined with euphoria and to negative affect when combined with the anger-eliciting situation. This condition showed that both adrenaline and the interpretation of the situation *combined* were sufficient conditions for eliciting an emotion. Moreover, the situation determined which emotion the participants felt.

However, when adrenaline was injected and its effect explained beforehand, the participants did not report an emotion. The participants knew that the drug would make their hands shake, their heart pound, and their face get warm, and they did not look for information in the situation that could explain their state. The situation did not give rise to an emotion because they could explain their physiological arousal. Another group was misinformed about the effects; these participants were told that the drug may cause numbness in their feet, an itching sensation in parts of the body, and a slight headache. As predicted by the two-factor theory, these participants felt an emotion. The alleged effects of the drug did not correspond to its actual effects. Therefore, physiological arousal remained unexplained and participants had to search for a source of their state; they only felt an emotion after they had used information from the environment.

For decades, the two-factor theory was the most influential explanation of the emergence of emotion, and it inspired many empirical studies on the misattribution of arousal to emotion. In one study, men were interviewed after crossing a wobbly bridge over a deep gorge that tilted and swayed and thus elicited arousal and fear. The interviewer was either a man or a woman. At the end, the interviewer offered the phone number so that the participants could call to ask about the results of the study. When the interviewer was a woman, many more men accepted the phone number and called than when the interviewer was a man. Moreover, the men who crossed the bridge were given the picture of a pensive woman and had to provide an interpretation. When interviewed by a woman, men gave more sexually colored interpretations than when interviewed by a man. Apparently, the men misattributed arousal from crossing a wobbly bridge to the sexual attraction of the woman who interviewed them (Dutton & Aron, 1974).

The main criticism of the two-factor theory is that it explains a situation that is rare in everyday life. A person rarely feels arousal but does not know why. The more usual situation seems to be that a person perceives a situation and appraises it. This appraisal then leads to physiological arousal and the feeling of an emotion (Reisenzein, 1983).

While the two-factor theory considers an emotion as the cognitive interpretation of physiological activation, *appraisal theories* define emotion as including multiple components. One of the best-known appraisal theories has been developed by Klaus Scherer (1984). He assumed that each emotion includes a cognitive component, a physiological component, a feeling component, an expressive component, and an action tendency. Each component serves a specific function. The cognitive component supports the evaluation of the environment; the physiological component the regulation of the bodily system; the feeling component reflection on and monitoring of mental states; the expressive component the communication of emotion to the outside world; and the action tendency the preparation of the behavioral response.

In appraisal theories of emotion, the interpretation of the situation (the cognitive component) determines the quality of an emotion, which is in line with the two-factor theory. The same situation might be interpreted in different ways and therefore result in different emotions. However, going beyond predictions of the two-factor theory, appraisal theorists could rely on evidence that the cognitive interpretation of a situation influences physiological arousal. Such findings contradicted the notion of the two-factor theory that physiological arousal comes first and its cognitive interpretation second.

In a well-known study (Speisman, Lazarus, Mordkoef, & Davison, 1964), participants saw a movie about a genital mutilation ritual. The soundtrack encouraged one group of participants to watch the movie from the detached perspective of a scientist interested in the technicalities of the event. A second group was encouraged to deny the harm and pain done by the ritual. Participants taking the perspective of a scientist or denying the harmful consequences showed less physiological responses to the movie than a third group that watched the movie with a soundtrack that emphasized the traumatic consequences of the ritual. Interpreting the event as a scientific phenomenon or denying negative consequences decreased physiological arousal and the intensity of emotion.

Appraisal theorists assume that individuals do not only interpret the situation as positive or negative but ask whether they can achieve their goals or alleviate threats through their actions, which is called *coping potential*. Let us look at an example. What is the difference between anger and fear when it is directed toward another person? In both emotions, a person perceives an intentional threat by someone else, a negative state that disrupts ongoing activity and the pursuit of a goal. So far, anger and fear are based on similar appraisals. The difference lies in coping potential. When a person thinks that she has the potential to cope with the threat by the other one, she will feel anger that includes an action tendency to attack. If she thinks she lacks coping potential, like Liza when she is seeing a dog, she will experience fear that includes an action tendency to withdraw. In line with the action tendencies, the facial and bodily expression of anger and fear differ. Expression and posture of anger prepare people to move forward and attack, while expression and posture of fear prepare them to move backward and withdraw.

From early observations that typical facial expressions of distinct emotions are recognized around the world and therefore seem to be a universal (Ekman & Friesen, 1971), theorists postulated the existence of *basic emotions* that have a biological basis and are clearly distinct.

Examples of basic emotions are joy, anger, fear, sadness, and disgust. However, the assumption that there are basic emotions encountered some difficulties. They lack clear limits that distinguish them from each other. Despite the early observations, it is far from clear that facial expressions of emotions and their recognition by other people are the same across cultures; some emotions, such as hope or guilt, do not even have a clearly recognizable facial expression.

In order to overcome such difficulties, theorists like Russell (2003) challenged this biological view and claimed that there are no basic emotions; feeling states can be explained by *core affect* that consists of two dimensions: pleasantness and activation. Every emotion can be depicted within this two-dimensional affective space. When we experience a feeling, human language labels it according to its pleasantness and activation level. For example, both anger and sadness are negative but anger represents a more activated feeling state than sadness.

Let us come back to William James' question: what is an emotion? We have seen that the James-Lange theory is wrong – emotions are not simply feelings derived from physiological states. The two-factor theory of emotion is not necessarily wrong but explains an exceptional situation where people are aroused without knowing why. It is more usual that people appraise a situation before they get aroused and feel an emotion. Finally, the notion that universal basic emotions are rooted in our biology has been challenged by theorists who claim that core affect consists of two dimensions, pleasantness and activation, and we use emotion terms to label these states. It remains to be seen whether future research can find more definitive biological origins of distinct emotions that falsifies the idea that emotions are just labels.

POSITIVE AND NEGATIVE EMOTIONS

Some psychologists have followed William James in asking, "What is an emotion?" In contrast, others have been interested in individual emotions, such as joy, anger, or fear. We shall discuss each of these emotions. The section on joy and happiness will review the role of positive emotions for happiness; the discussion of anger will be embedded in the frustration-aggression hypothesis; the discussion of fear contrasts explanations in terms of the appraisal theory with the assumption that humans have a fear module in the brain.

Joy and happiness

People feel joy about a positive event, for example winning a medal at a sports event or the birth of a child. A state related to joy is happiness. What makes people happy? In order to respond to this question, we have to know what happiness is, which is difficult because there are at least four definitions: the first based on objective measures of the satisfaction of needs, the second on subjective measures of the satisfaction of desires, the third on feelings of well-being that may be independent of satisfaction of needs or desires, and the final on being a good person that flourishes (see Annas, 2011).

First, economists try to define happiness objectively, for example, through income, life expectation, health services, level of education, and low crime rates. The definition is reminiscent of the satisfaction of needs as defined by Maslow and introduces objective measures to assess these needs. An objective definition is useful to assess the average happiness of nations but it is a coarse measure of the happiness of individuals and does not consider subjective factors, such as whether a person thinks her needs are fulfilled or whether she indeed feels happy.

The second definition focuses on happiness as the fulfillment of desires. If you want to become a millionaire and you achieve this goal, you are happy. Such an account of happiness would predict a positive correlation between income and happiness (for an explanation of correlation, see Box 3.1).

Box 3.1 What is correlation?

There is a saying that money does not buy happiness. Is this true? In order to study this question, a researcher may recruit a sample of adult people and collect data on income and happiness. While it may be relatively straightforward to assess income, it is more difficult to assess happiness as there are several ways to define the term.

After data collection, the researcher has one score for income and one score for happiness for each person. Let us look at Table 3.1 that depicts different hypothetical outcomes for 10 adults (in reality, researchers need to collect data from many more people).

The statistical relationship between income and happiness – or any two variables – is called *correlation*. It can be quantified by computing a *correlation coefficient* which provides a numerical estimate of the strength of the relationship. The correlation coefficient, often abbreviated *r*, ranges from −1 to +1 (or 1), where 1 means a perfect positive relationship between two variables, −1 a perfect negative relationship, and 0 no relationship at all.

Table 3.1 Outcomes of correlation analyses for three hypothetical cases

Correlation:	*Positive*	*Negative*	*Low*
Annual Income	*Happiness*	*Happiness*	*Happiness*
23,200	5.5	9.7	7.3
29,000	6.6	9.8	6.3
37,800	7.6	9.1	7.4
45,900	6.2	8.5	9.2
51,100	8.3	8.4	6.4
55,800	8.6	8.2	4.7
61,400	8.9	7.1	8.7
66,100	8.7	8.0	5.8
70,300	9.5	6.5	8.4
79,000	9.8	5.2	6.9
Correlation with Income:	0.92	−0.94	0.01

Note: Income could be in US dollars, British pounds, or euros; happiness ratings from 0 (not at all happy) to 10 (very happy).

As you can see, in the column labeled "positive," the higher the income, the higher is happiness, at least roughly. In other words, income is positively related to happiness, or – more technically – income scores and happiness scores are positively correlated. The correlation coefficient is $r = 0.92$, which is a very high positive correlation. The reverse is true in the next column where the correlation coefficient is negative. As you can see, the higher the income, the lower is happiness; the correlation coefficient is $r = -0.94$, which is a very high negative correlation. In the rightmost column, there is not much of a relationship between income and happiness; the correlation is close to zero, $r = 0.01$.

It is important to note that correlation is not causation; that is, when we have a positive correlation between income and happiness, we cannot conclude that an increase in income causes an increase in happiness. It could be the other way round, that is, happy people may earn more. It may even be that income and happiness influence each other; that is, people who earn more are happier and happier people in turn work better, which increases their income and so forth. Finally, a third variable could cause both income and happiness to increase. Such a third variable could be health. People in good health may earn more and be happier. In this case, income does not influence happiness and happiness does not influence income; the two variables are correlated because they have a common cause, in our example health.

I used for this illustration hypothetical data. In reality, income and happiness correlate positively, albeit not as strongly as in our hypothetical example and only up to a certain point. Thus, money can buy happiness only up to a certain point.

Indeed, there is a positive correlation between income and happiness up to an income of about US$75,000 (Kahneman & Deaton, 2010); at higher incomes, the correlation between income and happiness is close to zero. Apparently, when a person has an income to satisfy her daily needs, the satisfaction of further desires does not make her happier.

In surveys, happiness is often measured by asking for a person's well-being, which leads to the third definition. Defining happiness through personal well-being does not consider the satisfaction of some objective needs or subjective desires but assumes that the important aspect of happiness is how a person feels.

The fourth definition takes up the ancient question whether a person could be happy without leading a morally good life. Based on Aristotle's claim that happiness and virtue are intertwined, proponents of positive psychology defined happiness in terms of flourishing. Positive psychology emerged as a movement that countered the prevailing focus of psychology, and especially clinical psychology, on alleviating negative states. Instead, positive psychology aims to build a strong person who is resilient in the face of adversities, which can be achieved by mustering people's strengths and increasing frequency and intensity of positive states (Fredrickson, 2001).

The consequences of frustration

In general, people feel positive affect when everything is going smoothly. Indeed, most people are happy most of the time (Diener & Diener, 1996). Negative emotions occur when the normal course of action is interrupted. For example, the normal course of action for a girl is to ask her father for food, and she gets it. However, if the girl wants to have a candy in the supermarket and the father says no, the normal course of action is interrupted because he denies the fulfillment of his daughter's specific desire. Consequently, the child gets frustrated.

A well-known hypothesis, going back to Sigmund Freud, states that frustration – defined as blockage of desired goals – leads to aggression (Dollard, Miller, Doob, Mowrer, & Sears, 1939). This hypothesis fits the earlier mentioned notion that aggression may be the result from an appraisal that another person prevents us from reaching a desired goal but we have the potential to cope with the situation. This appraisal results in the feeling of anger and prepares the person to attack. Despite ample evidence for the frustration-aggression hypothesis (see Berkowitz, 1989), psychologists learned the lesson that evidence for the existence of an effect does not mean that the effect is universal. Soon after Dollard and colleagues published their work, Barker, Dembo, and Lewin (1941) showed that children who get frustrated may fall back (or *regress*) to a behavior from an earlier stage in their development. So there were two hypotheses, the *frustration-aggression hypothesis* and the *frustration-regression hypothesis*. Later observation of children in everyday situations showed that in fact, (1) children are not often frustrated, and (2) when frustrated, children most often showed no reaction to frustration – neither aggression nor regression (Fawl, 1963). What we can learn from such findings is that psychological states usually have various consequences. Likewise, a certain behavior may have various antecedents. When we look at the young smoker's aggression at the subway station, we may be tempted to assume that he must have been frustrated. However, his aggression might have other causes, such as pleasure of demonstrating dominance. Similarly, an SS guard who killed victims in a concentration camp was not necessarily frustrated but killed because he obeyed an authority that had ordered it; an issue we explore in Chapter 7.

Fear

Appraisal theories of emotion assume that the interpretation and appraisal of the situation determines an emotion. They plausibly derive an emotion from higher-order cognitive processes, such as thoughts, interpretations, and judgments. However, it seems strange that such complex cognitive processes determine basic emotions, given that animals like cats and dogs express fear.

As discussed earlier in this chapter, appraisal theorists assumed that fear results from a process where people appraise a situation in terms of a threat that they cannot cope with. In recent decades, neuroscientists have assumed that humans and animals have a fear module that gets activated immediately. This is possible because of a fast neural pathway to the amygdala, an important center in the brain for the processing of emotions. When a person sees a snake, the information goes to the thalamus where perceptual information is forwarded on two pathways: a fast one directly to the amygdala and a slow one to the visual cortex, where the incoming information is processed in order to determine what kind of object it is. Hence, information that potential danger is imminent gets to the amygdala before a person knows that it is a snake (see LeDoux, 1996). As it is important to react fast, the fear module is built to avoid misses and therefore accepts a high rate of false alarms (see Box 2.1). Given that you might die if you are bitten once from a snake, you do not mind if the object that frightens you turns out to be a stick.

Recommended literature

Overview

Frijda, N.H. (1988). The laws of emotion. *American Psychologist, 43*, 349–358.

Classical primary sources

Deci (1971; see references).
Schachter & Singer (1962; see references).

BRAIN AND GENES

The fear module discussed in the last section of Chapter 3 is part of the brain. Behavior, thought, and feeling in general are embedded in human biology. In the first section, we discuss the relationship between brain and mind. The second section presents methods of brain imaging and mentions briefly the biochemical basis of mental processes. The final section looks at how biologists and psychologists determine to what degree behavior and mental capacities are inherited.

BRAIN AND MIND

At the end of the previous chapter, we have seen that brain processes help explain why we are scared of a snake and recoil from it before we know whether it is a snake. There are two elements in this situation: the activation of the amygdala and the experience of fear. The question arises how activation of the amygdala could give rise to the experience of fear. More generally, how can a brain process lead to a mental process? On the other hand, I may have the intention to go to the kitchen and I begin to move my legs. How could an intention activate the brain areas that control muscles? More generally, how could a mental process influence brain processes? In modern psychology, there are two main views to look at the relationship between mental state and the brain: dualism and materialism.

Mind-brain dualism means that the mind and the brain are two separate entities. Fear and intentions belong to the mind, activation of the amygdala or areas that control muscles to the brain. Mind-brain dualism is popular but raises problems. The hard question is how a mental state could translate into a brain process and vice versa (Chalmers, 1996). There are no known mechanisms that could explain how activation of the amygdala could result in the feeling of fear and how an intention to move translates into nervous signals that activate the muscles.

As it seems impossible to answer the question how mental states and brain states can interact (the hard question), some theorists think that there is nothing like a mental state. What we label "seeing," "thinking," and "feeling" in everyday language are nothing else than brain states. This view, called *materialism*, assumes that all mental processes are by-products of brain processes and can be explained in biochemical terms. As mental processes are reduced to biological processes, this view is also called *biological reductionism*.

Psychological research has addressed questions pertaining to the interaction of mind and body. Let us look at two examples: the first is about the relationship between intentions and preparation of a movement in the brain, which also relates to the question of free will; the second is about the role of expectancies in pain relief, which relates to the placebo effect.

It is a commonsense assumption that people have an intention and then act on it. For example, Deborah first has an intention to move her finger and then moves her finger. However, the hard question is how Deborah's intention can make her finger move. A classical study has been conducted by Benjamin Libet (1985). His participants sat in front of a clock with a pointer that moved round very fast. He instructed the participants to tell at which position of the pointer they had the intention to move the finger. At the same time, he measured so-called readiness potentials. These are brain signals related to the preparation of the movement. With this technique, Libet could compare the time point at which Deborah had the intention to the time point at which she started to prepare the movement. From everyday experience, we would expect that Deborah first has the intention to move the finger and then the brain prepares the command to actually perform the movement. In contrast to this commonsense assumption, Libet found that the preparation for movement started more than 300 milliseconds before the intention! This finding led some psychologists and philosophers to conclude that free will is an illusion. According to this view, humans think they first have an intention and then act; in fact, the action is predetermined and the intention just an *epiphenomenon*, that is, an event that has no further influence on our actions. However, Libet (1985) also found that participants could change the course of action about 150 milliseconds after the conscious intention had appeared, which means that the preparation for action does not preclude later correction. The theoretical discussion on whether humans have free will is still ongoing.

At a more practical level, we might ask, how can my mere expectation that a painkiller is effective alleviate my pain? Even if the doctor is giving me a placebo that does not contain any ingredient to reduce pain, I may feel less pain after I swallowed the pill. This placebo effect can be explained in two ways. First, through classical conditioning; already Ivan Pavlov (1927) reported a colleague's observation that a dog had to vomit after morphine injections. When the experimenter prepared the syringe and touched the dog but before any morphine was injected, the dog again produced severe nausea. In the terminology introduced in Chapter 1, morphine was the US that produced vomiting (UR). The mere sight of the syringe (CS) was sufficient to elicit vomiting again (CR). Later research confirmed that classical conditioning could explain placebo effects. To come back to the question at the beginning of the paragraph, if I swallow a substance (US) that reduces my pain (UR), then I notice form and color of the pill (CS). If I get a placebo pill that looks like the painkiller (CS), it nevertheless reduces pain (CR).

Besides classical conditioning, expectations contribute to the placebo effect. To disentangle conditioning and expectation, Montgomery and Kirsch (1997) induced pain to the skin by means of electrical current and then applied a cream. Unbeknownst to the participants, when the experimenters applied the cream, they also reduced the current so that the cream unfailingly reduced pain and thus became a CS. In one condition, the participants were told about the experimental setup. When participants knew that the experimenter reduced pain at the same moment the ineffective cream was applied, no placebo effect occurred. This means that an automatic conditioned response was overridden by expectancy. This and later studies did not exclude the possibility that classical conditioning produces placebo effects but the most plausible mechanism includes expectancies.

Nevertheless, neither the observation by Libet (1985) nor the studies on the placebo effect solve the hard problem of consciousness – how thoughts influence brain processes. If we adhere to mind-brain dualism, there must be some unknown mechanisms that translate thoughts in the mind into processes in the nervous system. Alternatively, biological reductionists may define thoughts in terms of biological processes so that translation is not necessary.

METHODS OF COGNITIVE BRAIN RESEARCH

Cognitive psychologists had a hard time to come up with experimental techniques to examine the mind. However, for a long time, it had also been difficult to examine the brain. The earliest method was the examination of the consequences of brain damage through stroke or injury. In the 1860s and 1870s, physiologists found areas in the *left hemisphere* of the brain – which is the left half of the brain – dedicated to language production and language understanding. Some patients with a damaged *Broca's area* showed an inability to produce speech but were able to understand language. Patients with a damaged *Wernicke's area* were able to produce speech but they were unable to understand language (for brain areas mentioned in the text, see Figure 4.1).

This is a *double dissociation*. While some patients suffer from deficits of language production with intact language understanding, others suffer from deficits in understanding but their production of speech is intact. This observation suggests that two different systems underlie language production and language understanding. Double dissociations play an important role in showing that two functions are served by two different brain systems.

Studies of patients with brain damage allowed localization of some functions, such as the *occipital lobe* – which is the rear part of the brain – for visual perception or the *frontal lobe* – which is the front part of the brain – for *executive functions* that enable people to plan ahead, control their behavior, and think new thoughts. People with

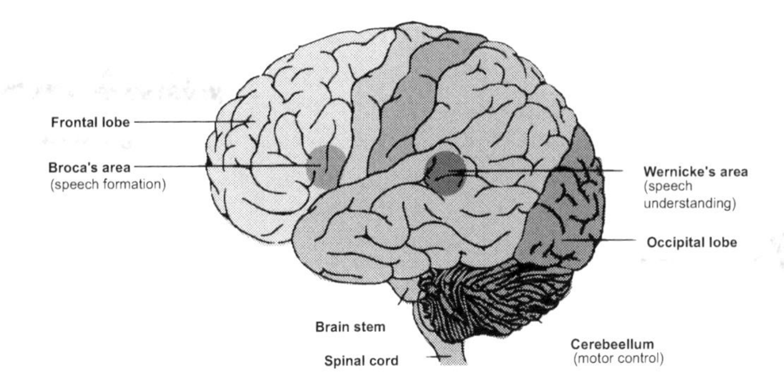

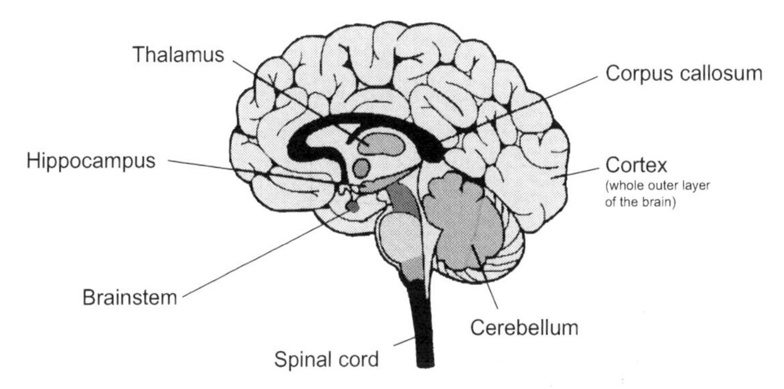

Figure 4.1 Structures of the brain, seen from the left. The upper panel shows the brain from the outside the lower panel is a section through the middle of the brain such that the two brain hemispheres are separated.

deficits in executive functions often act impulsively because they are unable to inhibit thought and action and to resist temptation.

Although brain damage yielded new insights into the brain's function, it has several drawbacks. First, naturally occurring lesions of the human brain are rarely limited to one clearly circumscribed area but often encompass several areas and have fuzzy boundaries.

It is therefore often unclear whether deficits of perception, thought, or language are caused by a destroyed area, by partly damaged areas in the neighborhood of the destroyed area, or by severed nerve tracts that connect a brain area with sensory organs or other brain areas.

Second, it is unethical to inflict brain lesions in humans for the sake of conducting research. Therefore, brain scientists had to rely on animal studies or on brain surgeries performed for medical reasons. A classical study in rats has demonstrated loss of memory when the *cortex* – the outer layer of the brain – is lacking. Therefore, memory must be stored somewhere in the cortex. Karl Lashley (1950) wanted to know where in the cortex memories were stored, or – in his terminology – where the *memory engram* was located. In his experiments, rats learned to find food in a maze. Then he removed a specific part of a rat's cortex. Afterwards, he tested whether the rat was still was able to find the location of food in the maze. At the end of his studies, he had removed each part of the cortex without finding one specific area where memory for the food in the maze disappeared. Lashley concluded that memory did not depend on a specific location in the brain but is distributed across the cortex.

In humans, brain surgery was used to contain severe epilepsy. Surgeons tried to limit the propagation of seizures by removing clearly defined areas of the brain. In one such surgery, Scoville and Milner (1957) removed parts of the hippocampi and adjacent areas on both sides of the brain of a patient, Henry Molaison, who came to be known by his initials H.M. Removal of these areas helped with the seizures but had a severe side effect: H.M. could not acquire new memories. It became clear that the *hippocampus* is essential for memory formation, a finding supported by numerous further studies. As soon as it became clear what severe effects the removal of the hippocampus has, neurologists abandoned this surgery.

Another surgery aimed to prevent seizures from passing from one brain hemisphere to the other. To this purpose, surgeons cut nerve fibers in the *corpus callosum* which connects the two hemispheres. When we look straight ahead, the information we see on the left side (the left *visual hemifield*) is processed in the right hemisphere of the brain, and information on the right side (the right visual hemifield) in the left hemisphere. Similarly, movements by the left hand are controlled by brain areas in the right hemisphere, and movements by the right hand in the left hemisphere. Such crossing over is typical for the processing of both sensory information – what we see, hear, or feel by touch – and motor information that guide movements. Moreover, language production and understanding is located in the left hemisphere. *Split-brain experiments* with patients who lacked the corpus callosum provided deeper insights into the *laterality* of the brain, which denotes the fact that some functions, most prominently language, are located on one side of the brain.

In a typical split-brain experiment, a patient without corpus callosum sits in front of a screen, with different objects hidden behind the screen so that the patient cannot see the objects but can reach them with his hands. A word, for example HAMMER, is briefly presented on the left side of the screen and thus in the left visual hemifield. The patient focuses on a fixation point at the center of the screen such that the information about the briefly flashed word is processed in the right hemisphere of the brain. However, as the information cannot pass the corpus callosum, it does not reach the language centers in the left hemisphere. If the experimenter asks the patient what he has seen, he responds, "I don't know." Yet when the experimenter asks to give her the object with the left hand, the patient reaches for the hammer. As the information from the left side of the screen enters the right hemisphere which controls the movements of the left hand, information does not have to cross the two hemispheres and the patient is perfectly able to find the correct object. When the word BALL is presented on the right side of the screen and thus in the right visual hemifield, the information is transmitted to the left hemisphere where it reaches the language areas. This time, the patient is able to tell the experimenter that he saw the word BALL. This experiment confirms the observation from brain lesion studies that language understanding is lateralized, that is, located in one side of the brain, here the left hemisphere.

There was a third disadvantage of relying on naturally occurring brain lesions. For a long time, the precise location of brain lesions could not be determined in a living human. While laboratory animals were killed after an experiment to check the precise location of a lesion, the brains of human patients were dissected only after their natural death. For example, after Alois Alzheimer observed the clinical characteristics of dementia in his patient Auguste Deter in 1901, he was only able to detect the damage of Deter's brain after she died in 1906. Thanks to brain imaging techniques, diagnostics of brain damage has dramatically improved.

Structural brain imaging, for example magnetic resonance imaging (MRI), provides information about the structure of the brain at rest. This technique is used in diagnoses of brain damage caused by conditions like Alzheimer's disease, brain injury, or stroke.

An important technique for psychological research is *functional magnetic resonance imaging* (fMRI). The basic principle is to measure the energy used in certain parts of the brain during an activity, such as looking at pictures, listening to sounds, or making plans. When the brain works, it uses oxygen, especially in the most active brain regions. The level of oxygen in the blood inside the brain can be measured and is an indicator of the energy used during an activity. Brain imaging techniques are often used to measure where the brain is most active during an activity. It can be shown, for example, that visual information is processed in the occipital lobe and memory formation is related to activity in the hippocampus. These studies confirmed and extended with a new technique what has been shown in earlier lesion studies and animal research.

The arguably most useful function of brain imaging techniques is its use to address open theoretical questions. For example, why is it easier for early bilinguals to speak a second language they have learned as a young child than for late bilinguals who have learned the second language in high school or as adults? One hypothesis states that early bilinguals have a single "place" or entry in their memories for concepts in both languages, whereas late bilinguals have two entries for the same concept in the two languages. Assume that Maria describes an event from the previous day, first in English and then in Spanish. If she is an early bilingual, she accesses the same entry for both the English and the Spanish description. By contrast, late bilinguals would have to access two distinct entries to describe the same event in English and in Spanish. Such a hypothesis is difficult to test with the methods used in cognitive psychology. However, with neuroscientific methods, it is possible to observe whether the processing of two languages is located in overlapping or distinct regions of the brain. Using fMRI, Kim, Relkin, Lee, and Hirsch (1997) measured activation in Broca's area, which is related to speech production, when participants described an event from the previous day; before each trial, participants received a signal in which of two languages they had to recount the event. For early bilinguals, the description in both languages was related to activation in overlapping regions of Broca's area. For late bilinguals, by contrast, the description in the two languages was related to activation in adjacent but clearly distinct brain regions. This study suggests that learning a second language early results in common entries for both languages whereas learning a second language late results in distinct entries for the two languages.

Brain imaging techniques have the advantage that they have high spatial resolution so that we get a sharp image of brain segments as small as 1 cubic millimeter. However, these techniques have the drawback that their temporal resolution is low. For example, fMRI can measure brain activity that lasts 1 second or more. Low temporal resolution is a problem because much of the processing of incoming stimuli happens within the first 500 milliseconds.

Luckily, researchers who need high temporal resolution to explore brain processes have the option to use *event-related potential* (ERP). This method was developed from *electroencephalography* (EEG), which measures electric signals stemming from the brain on the surface of the skull. EEG has been used since the 1930s to measure brain activity, most prominently in sleep research where different wave forms of the electric signals have been identified that indicate different stages of sleep.

ERP measures electrical brain activity while an event occurs. When a stimulus event occurs, for example, when a person sees a surprising object, there is a slight change in brain activity that can be measured. A typical experiment is the *oddball paradigm*, in which the participant has to detect an event that is different from others. An example is a 2,000 Hz tone in a train of 1,000 Hz tones. The ERP response is more pronounced around 300 ms after the onset of the 2,000 Hz tones than after the onset of the 1,000 Hz tones. This specific response is called P300 and occurs when a person has to detect irregular stimuli, such as the 2,000 Hz tone among the usual 1,000 Hz tone. The detection of abnormalities in the environment is important for survival. Humans are therefore equipped with attentional processes to detect irregular stimuli in the stream of the usual stimuli. ERP, combined with attentional tasks like the oddball paradigm, enables researchers to examine in the laboratory a mental process that is essential for survival in nature.

The drawback of ERP is its limited spatial resolution, so that it is difficult to determine the location of electrical activity. Researchers can only tell whether an activity happens in the left or right hemisphere or in the front or the rear of the brain. It has become possible to combine fMRI with ERP in order to get the best out of both methods: high spatial resolution from fMRI and high temporal resolution from ERP. These methods are difficult to implement and expensive, but they will certainly improve cognitive brain research in the future.

Methods to measure brain activity have not only been used to explore the connection between brain and behavior but also to help patients with locked-in syndrome, which is a state in which patients appear to be awake but show no signs of awareness. Such states may be seen in patients who emerge from a coma or suffer from a disease, such as amyotrophic lateral sclerosis (ALS). In ALS, nerve cells that innervate muscles degenerate. The patients can neither speak nor use their muscles to operate communication devices or even to signal to their relatives that they are conscious. There are two ways to help these patients communicate with the outer world.

One method applies brain imaging. In healthy individuals, an area called the supplementary motor cortex is activated when they imagine playing tennis. This area is also active when people actually play tennis. The parahippocampal gyrus, a brain area surrounding the hippocampus, is activated when people imagine navigating through their house. This area is associated to navigation and scene processing. Adrian Owen and colleagues (2006) examined a woman who was involved in a traffic accident some months before the experiment that left her in a vegetative state. As she was unable to move any part of the body, there were no outer signs of awareness. For the study, Owen and colleagues placed the patient in a brain scanner and told her to imagine playing tennis. Indeed, the supplementary motor cortex was activated. When asked to imagine that she walks through the rooms of her house, the parahippocampal gyrus was activated. This was a first sign that the woman was conscious. Later studies revealed that the same brain imaging method could be used to answer "yes" or "no" questions. One patient even showed that he recorded new memories. When asked whether his sister has a daughter, the patient answered "yes"; as his niece was born after he fell into a vegetative state, this is evidence that he could understand and record new memories.

Another application that allows patients suffering from locked-in syndrome to communicate uses EEG technology. To some extent, people can be trained to influence the pattern of electrophysiological activation, which can be measured and translated into a response, for example the selection of a letter. By influencing the brain response, locked-in patients can write a message letter by letter. Although this process is very slow – writing speed is two to three letters per minute – it is often the only way a patient is able communicate to the outside world (Birbaumer et al., 1999).

The examples of research with patients suffering from locked-in syndrome show that researchers can use methods to measure brain activity to develop tools that assist people in new ways.

Let me briefly mention that another route to explore the biological basis of behavior and mind is to link mental processes to biochemistry. Researchers in this field examine the relationship of hormones or chemical processes in the brain to behavior, thought, and feeling.

Let us come back to the notion of materialism. How far have we come in explaining the mind in terms of the brain? The answer is not very far. To date, neither anatomical structure nor biochemical processes could explain mental processes, and we still do not know how a certain thought could be translated into a particular neural signature.

GENES AND BEHAVIOR

Whether a young man attacks a subway employee who rebukes him for his smoking, Liza is afraid of dogs, or George has learning difficulties, laypeople often assume that such behavior is inherited. In the aforementioned nature-nurture debate, they take the stance that behavior is determined by the nature of the person.

Traits – which are predispositions to behave in a characteristic way – are transmitted from one generation to the next by *genes*, which are the carriers of hereditary information. The genetic information about some physical attributes like eye color (blue or brown) is coded on one gene. Each parent transmits one gene to the child, either for brown or blue eye color. The two genes from each parent make up the *genotype* for eye color. As the brown eye color is the dominant gene, a child will have brown eyes if at least one gene codes brown eyes. That is, if both father *and* mother each transmit a brown eye gene, or if either father *or* mother transmits a brown eye gene, the child will have brown eyes. Although there may be different genotypes, either two genes for brown eyes or one gene for brown eyes and one for blue eyes, the *phenotype* is the same; phenotype relates to outer appearance – as eye color in our example – but also to biological functioning or behavioral traits. Only if both parents transmit the blue eye gene (genotype) will the child have blue eyes (phenotype). This kind of genetic transmission is straightforward; a child has either brown eyes or blue eyes, and this information is coded on a single gene.

When it comes to behavioral traits, inheritance is not as straightforward. There is no single gene that transmits the disposition to depression such that an offspring either has depression or not. In general, behavioral traits are not coded on one gene. According to the best explanation for transmission of behavioral traits to date, information about behavioral dispositions is coded on clusters of genes that together result in a tendency to show a certain disposition, such as early onset Alzheimer's disease or addiction. Recent research has shown that most neurological diseases, like Alzheimer's disease and Parkinson's disease, can be clearly distinguished based on their genetic makeup. This suggests that they have independent neurological causes. By contrast, most psychological disorders, such as depression, schizophrenia, and anxiety, cannot be distinguished by their genetic makeup and do not seem to be independent diseases (Anttila et al., 2018). The problems of classifying psychological disorders plague psychiatry and clinical psychology to this day (see Chapter 8).

How can we find out whether behavior or a disorder is genetically transmitted? A quirk of nature helps researchers disentangle the contributions of genes and the environment. There are two kinds of twins: identical or *monozygotic twins*, who share all their genes; and fraternal or *dizygotic twins*, who share on average 50 percent of their genes, which is the same proportion as siblings who are not twins. In theory, as monozygotic twins share all genes, any difference between them must come from the environment, which includes influences from family, school, food, and intellectual enrichment through books and toys. There is a complication, though. Parents may create more similar environments for monozygotic twins than for dizygotic twins. To make environments comparable, researchers examined twins who were adopted into different families in so-called *twin adoption studies*. If we assume that the placement of the infants accorded to the same rules for both kinds of twins, environments for monozygotic and dizygotic twins should be the same on average.

To know to what degree intelligence is inherited, researchers examined the intelligence of monozygotic and dizygotic twins reared apart. They then computed the correlation between the first and the second twin – if one twin of a pair scores high on intelligence, does the second one also tend to score high? If intelligence were genetically determined, we would expect that monozygotic twins have more similar intelligence scores than dizygotic twins, that is, the correlation of intelligence scores between monozygotic twins is higher than the correlation of scores between dizygotic twins (correlation was explained in Box 3.1).

From the difference between these two correlations, we can calculate *heritability*, which measures the genetic component within a population (for example, all adults in the United States or all adolescents in the United Kingdom). For intelligence, heritability explains around 50 percent. Intelligence differs among individuals within a population, and this value means that 50 percent of these differences in intelligence can be explained by genetic factors. By this definition, heritability does not mean to what degree intelligence in an individual is due to genetic factors; you cannot claim that 50 percent of your intelligence is inherited. If the correlation of scores between pairs of monozygotic and dizygotic twins were similar, we could conclude that there is no or only a small and thus undetectable genetic component. By contrast, twin adoption studies showed that genetic influences explain up to 50 percent of the differences among individuals for intelligence, personality traits, and psychological disorders, such as schizophrenia, depression, and alcohol dependence. This also means that the environment explains 50 percent and more of individual differences in behavioral dispositions.

Even if a behavioral disposition is genetically transmitted, the environment plays a crucial role in whether this behavior becomes manifest. There are at least three ways how the environment may interact with genetic information (for an overview, see Holt et al., 2015).

First, the environment may influence heritability. Consider height. Where all children have adequate nutrition, heritability will be high; environment plays virtually no role because it is optimal for every child. However, where food is scarce and nutrition insufficient, height will depend on how much food a child gets. The role of environmental factors increases while the role of heritability decreases. Similar reasoning applies to intelligence, as Turkheimer, Haley, Waldron, D'Onofrio, and Gottesman (2003) have shown. In their study, intelligence depended on heritability when children came from affluent families. Environment played virtually no role because it is optimal for every child. By contrast, children from impoverished families differed in the intellectual stimulation they received. Therefore, the role of environmental factors increased and the role of heritability decreased.

Second, the environment may influence the expression of the behavior that has been genetically transmitted. Let us look at intelligence. What is genetically transmitted is not a precise intelligence quotient (IQ) but a *reaction range* within which intelligence could fall; for example, the genetically transmitted reaction range for a person may fall between an IQ of 110 and 130 (for what these scores mean, see Chapter 6). Let us assume that two children both inherit the same reaction range but one child lives in an enriched, intellectually stimulating environment and the other in a deprived environment without books, challenging games, and parents who talk with their children. When it comes to intelligence, it is very likely that the child from the enriched environment will be at the higher end of the reaction range than the child from the deprived environment. Moreover, a child from a deprived environment on average needs to have a reaction range with higher minimal and maximal values to show the same intelligence as a child from an enriched environment. There may be exceptions. For example, when a boy with a high reaction range in an enriched environment is bored and passive, he may show the same intelligence as a child from a deprived environment.

Third, genetic predisposition may influence the effects of the environment in at least three ways. First, genetic predisposition increases the likelihood that a child will grow up in an environment their parents have built up. For example, children with high inherited intelligence are more likely to live in an enriched environment because it is likely that their parents are already intelligent and create an enriched environment. Second, inherited traits may elicit responses from others. For example, adults may discuss more intellectual topics with an intelligent child than with a child with lower intellectual aptitude; this difference in the behavior of adults further increases the difference between intelligence scores. However, responses may also counter an inherited predisposition. For example, adults tend to calm down a hyperactive child or to stimulate a child that seems too passive. As temperament is inherited, the responses by adults counteract the genetically transmitted predisposition. Third, children select environments that are compatible with the inherited traits. For example, the hyperactive child is more likely to choose activities that match the need for activity, like sports or dance, whereas a calm child is more likely to choose activities like reading books or piecing together a jigsaw puzzle.

Can the environment influence genes? French biologist Jean-Baptiste Lamarck thought this was the case in the early 19th century. One of his examples was a giraffe with a short neck. As the giraffe has to eat leaves from high trees, it has to stretch the neck. Stretching the neck, Lamarck thought, might result in the inheritance of longer necks by its offspring (note that genes were unknown at the time of Lamarck). However, this view could not muster enough empirical support. It fell out of favor until recently when the field of epigenetics emerged. Yet we still know too little to be sure that the environment can influence genes related to behavior and mind.

Genes are transmitted from one generation to the next over hundreds and thousands of generations. Genetically transmitted information (the genotype) can change over the course of generations and result in changes of the expression of genes in the phenotype; this long-term process is called *evolution*. Let us come back to the evolution of the giraffe's neck. It is not necessary to assume that stretching the neck led to genetic changes that resulted in longer necks. According to evolutionary biologists in the tradition of Charles Darwin, two mechanisms suffice to explain the evolution of a trait across generations. First, spontaneous *mutation* means that genes undergo changes that remain permanent and may lead to changes in the phenotype, for example in longer necks of the giraffe. The second mechanism is *natural selection*, by which the genes of those traits are more likely to survive and reproduce when they are better adapted to the environment. Spontaneous mutation could result in the inheritance of harmful traits; the bearers of such detrimental mutations die out and the respective trait disappears. By contrast, when spontaneous mutation results in genetic change that is beneficial for survival in an environment, the bearers of these genes will be more likely to survive and reproduce. When we think of the giraffe example, the following scenario describes what most probably has happened. First, trees grew higher, and the giraffes with the longest necks were most likely to survive and transmit their genes to the next generation. Spontaneous mutation may have influenced neck length. If mutation led to shorter necks, the offspring died out and with them the genes that coded shorter necks. By contrast, if mutation led to longer necks, the probability increased that the animals survived and could transmit the gene. The mechanism – spontaneous mutation resulting in longer necks and natural selection for the animals with the longest neck – must have repeated several times, which resulted in giraffes having much longer necks than their ancestors once had. Similarly, mutation and natural selection may have shaped behavioral dispositions over the time of human evolution. For example, spontaneous mutation may have shaped anatomical structures in the brain and the vocal apparatus to enable humans to speak. These humans that were better able to communicate with each other thus had an advantage, for example because they could better plan group activities like hunting. According to evolutionary theory, natural selection led to survival of humans who could speak and to the demise of those who could not speak. We encounter another example of the notion of natural selection when we discuss an evolutionary account of mate choice in Chapter 7.

How can we know that human behavior evolved over the course of natural history? One indicator that human behavior is the product of evolution is that it is a universal. A human *universal* is an attribute that is shared by all human beings across cultures (see Norenzayan & Heine, 2005). By contrast, behavior that is specific for particular cultures is not universal and probably not the product of evolution based on genetic transmission. Examples of human universals are the ability to acquire spoken language and attachment of children to their mother or other caregivers. I later review universals in mate choice, language acquisition, and attachment in human development.

Recommended literature

Overviews

Gazzaniga, M., Ivry, R.B., & Mangun, G.R. (2013). *Cognitive neuroscience: The biology of the mind* (4th ed.). New York, NY: W.W. Norton.

Knopik, V.S., Neiderhiser, J.M., DeFries, J.C., & Plomin, R. (2016). *Behavioral genetics* (7th ed.). New York, NY: Worth.

Important primary sources

Kim et al. (1997; see references).
Owen et al. (2006; see references).

5

HUMAN DEVELOPMENT

In the first four chapters, we looked at determinants of behavior, such as learning, thoughts, emotions, and the brain. Such research is often done at one point in time with people of the same age. Instead of observing individuals at one time, developmental psychologists are interested in the change of mind and behavior across time, for example from infancy to adolescence.

WHAT IS DEVELOPMENT?

Development means directed change. We use developmental terms in everyday language, for example, "he is not mature enough," "she did not get enough love as a child," or "he was never taught to behave properly." The first term refers to maturation, the second to learning from experience, and the third to socialization. These are the three basic mechanisms underlying development.

Let us first discuss maturation. When George has difficulties learning a subject, parents often argue that the child is not mature enough. As often in psychology, the everyday use of a word is not as precise as its specific use in scientific language.

When psychologists use the term **maturation**, they mean **a process based on biological development**. Let us take physical growth. Every healthy child gains in height and weight; physical growth is universal. Growth shows a characteristic trajectory with growth spurts in early childhood and adolescence and lower growth rates in between. Finally, although environmental factors like nutrition or illness may advance or hamper growth, the process of development with growth spurts and relative stability is independent of such factors. These characteristics suggest that physical growth is a biological process and has a genetic basis.

Maturation plays a significant role in psychological development of the child. Brain development enables the growing child to store more information, to inhibit impulses, and to acquire language. Theories of psychological maturation often include stages, not just linear growth. *Stage theories* include four essential features. (1) The sequence of developmental steps is invariant and no stage can be skipped. After a babbling stage, a child utters single words. As the child already seems to make a statement – for example, "This is a bird" by uttering the word "Bird" – these utterances are sometimes called *one-word sentences*. This stage is followed by two-word sentences and later by sentences with three and more words. Stage theories assume that while the duration of a stage may depend on culture and family environment, the sequence of stages and their content are fixed. (2) A later stage builds on an earlier stage. In language development, for example, uttering two-word sentences builds on competence to utter one-word sentences. (3) The transition between stages includes a qualitative change. In language development, the change from one-word sentences to two word-sentences enables children to express qualitatively new meanings, such as connecting an action to a subject ("Bird fly") or to an object ("Drink milk"). (4) Stages are universal. The ability to learn to speak is a universal – one of the prerequisites for a biological process (Lenneberg, 1967). Every healthy child learns to speak. Universals only minimally depend on environmental influence.

Maturation sometimes includes a *critical period*, which is an age range at which the child needs some environmental stimulation for an ability to develop. If children are not exposed to any language until puberty, they miss the opportunity to learn language. This is the time when lateralization of the brain is completed; by puberty, language functions are definitely located in the left hemisphere. After puberty, it is very difficult if not impossible to learn to speak. The age until around 13 to 14 years is therefore considered the critical period to learn to speak (Lenneberg, 1967).

When we think of the critical period for learning a skill, such as language, we assume that children *gain* skills. Surprisingly, infants can lose skills through *perceptual narrowing* (for a review, see Maurer & Werker, 2014). For example, newborn infants have the potential to discriminate among speech sounds (so-called *phonemes*) from all languages. By 6 months of age, infants have learned to discriminate among speech sounds of their own language but have reduced ability to discriminate among speech sounds of other languages. The critical period to learn to discriminate among speech sounds of a language is up to around six months of age.

A striking example that children lose a skill through perceptual narrowing comes from a study on face perception. When infants repeatedly see the same face, it becomes familiar and looking times get shorter and shorter. This process is called ***habituation***. When presented with both a familiar and an unfamiliar face, infants look longer at the unfamiliar face. When two different but similar faces are shown, a previously seen one and a new one, researchers can observe whether infants recognize subtle differences by measuring looking times – children should look longer at the unfamiliar face. Pascalis, de Haan, and Nelson (2002) used not only human faces but also chimpanzee faces in their experiment. Infants up to 6 months were able to recognize subtle differences in both human and chimpanzee faces. By 9 months of age, children could recognize the subtle differences only in human faces but lost the ability to discriminate chimpanzee faces. At first, the child can recognize all kinds of faces. Later, children only recognize the kind of faces they have seen during the first months because it is most important for humans to recognize human faces, especially those in their own culture. Indeed, later research showed that by 9 months of age, children were best at recognizing faces of their own race (see Maurer & Werker, 2014).

To summarize, the first mechanism of development is maturation which denotes a biological process underlying growth. Growth usually is not linear but follows a sequence of stages. Finally, there may be critical periods of learning a skill, such as learning to speak. When that period has passed, the skill can be learned only with difficulty, if at all.

The second mechanism of development pertains to the influence of experience. According to the behaviorists, children learn by associating behavior with experienced outcomes – touching the fur of a cat is associated with pleasure, and touching a cup of hot tea with pain. We learn from firsthand experience throughout life, for example when we learn to ride a bicycle or to drive a car.

An ingenious study showed that experience begins before birth. A newborn child already prefers the voice of its mother. To explore this preference, the researchers exploited an ability newborns already have: regulating sucking frequency. They played the child two voices, the one of the mother and the voice of a woman unknown to the child (DeCasper & Fifer, 1980). Children could choose to hear the preferred voice by regulating the frequency of sucking a rubber nipple. It turned out that the infant preferred the voice of the mother to another woman's voice that in turn was preferred to male voices, regardless of whether it was the father's or another man's voice. Other studies showed that neonates prefer their native language (Mehler et al., 1988). The unborn fetus can already hear sounds in the mother's womb, and repeated exposure to the mother's voice or their native language results in preference for the familiar sounds. Such preference is present at birth but acquired through exposure to voices or language before birth.

The third mechanism of development, after maturation and experience, is social transmission. After touching a hot cup of tea, a child knows from experience that heat causes pain. Fortunately, children do not have to make firsthand experience with every source of heat; parents can simply tell them that a light bulb is hot, and (most) children will not touch it. Children learn not only from experience but also from being told about what to do, or about causes and effect. The process of acquiring the values, norms, beliefs, and ways of acting within a culture is called *socialization*. Indeed, developmental psychologists often debate whether development is universal, based on experience, or the result of socialization, as we shall see when we review theories of cognitive, emotional, and social development.

COGNITIVE DEVELOPMENT

The last 100 years brought enormous progress in our understanding of thinking and feeling in children. This section reports about the progress made in understanding cognitive development, most importantly by Piaget's stage theory of development that emerged between the 1920s and 1960s. The next section looks at emotional and social development.

Piaget divided cognitive development of children into four stages that build on each other: the sensorimotor, pre-operational, concrete-operational, and formal-operational stages.

During the *sensorimotor stage*, the child begins to differentiate between self and environment and between means and ends, which is important for intentional action. The most important accomplishment at the end of this stage is *object permanence*; that is, an object is seen as durable and existing even when one cannot view it. For younger infants, an object out of sight is no longer of interest, and children do not search for it. Some months later, infants may search for an object that is partially hidden or that has just been used, but they are easily distracted and give up the search. When proceeding through the sensorimotor stage, children begin to search for an object that disappears. Object permanence can be shown by mistakes children make. For example, Piaget tells the story of his son who saw a snail on the footpath and said, "Oh, look, a snail!" After walking some minutes, the child saw another snail and exclaimed, "Oh, look, the snail again!" Apparently, the child did not know that snails cannot move so fast and thought this must be the same snail. Clearly, the child had developed object permanence; else this mistake could not have happened.

The second stage is the *pre-operational stage*, in which children's thought is rigid and egocentric. Thought is *rigid* because children cannot take into account two aspects of a task at the same time, as shown by *conservation tasks*. Figure 5.1 shows two examples of such tasks – the upper panel for the *conservation of number* and the lower panel for the *conservation of volume*. For testing the understanding of conservation of number in children aged 3 to 8 years, the experimenter arranges one black row and one white row of checkers, with equal distances between checkers such that it is obvious that there are as many black checkers as white ones (upper panel, left). The experimenter then asks whether there are more white checkers, more black checkers, or an equal number of black and white checkers. Children at all ages answer that there are as many black checkers as white checkers. The experimenter then rearranges the row of white checkers such that the distances between the white checkers are smaller than the distances between the black checkers (upper panel, right). When asking the same question again, only children over the age of 5 or 6 thought that there were equal numbers

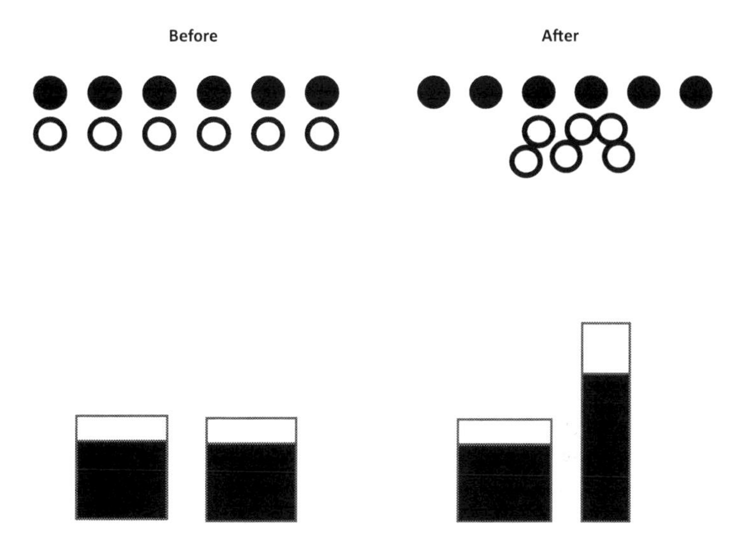

Figure 5.1 Conservation tasks. Upper panel: task to test conservation of number. Lower panel: task to test conservation of volume.

of black and white checkers; a majority of children below that age thought that there were more black checkers. These children did not understand that the number remains unchanged or invariant when the checkers are rearranged.

By the end of the pre-operational stage, children develop conservation across various dimensions. The development of the conservation of numbers is not an isolated phenomenon but one instance in a general development of the structure of thought from one stage to the other. Another well-known example is the water-level task, which tests the conservation of volume (Figure 5.1, lower panel). First, the experimenter presents the child with two identical glasses filled with the same amount of water and asks whether there is more water in one of the glasses or the same amount of water in both glasses. Children at all ages recognize that the two glasses contain the same amount of water. The child then observes how the experimenter pours the content of one of the glasses into another glass that is taller but narrower and then asks whether there is more water in one of the glasses or the same amount of water in both glasses. Only children over the age of 5 or 6 believed that the amount of water was the same in both glasses; a majority of children below that age stated that there was more water in the tall but narrow glass than in the short but wide one. Again, children's thought is rigid because they cannot simultaneously take two dimensions into account, and they do not recognize that volume of water is invariant when it is filled into a glass with different shape.

Piaget and Inhelder illustrated *egocentric thought* in children by the three mountains problem that measures *perspective taking*. This demonstration revealed that children at the pre-operational stage are not able to imagine the viewpoint of others. A child saw three mountains with different markers, such as snow in front of one of the mountains or a flag on another. The experimenter placed a doll at different points in the landscape and then showed the child several photographs. The child had to choose the one photograph that represented the viewpoint of the doll. In these studies, 3- to 4-year-old children pointed to the photograph that showed the landscape from their own viewpoint. Only children at age 7 or 8 were able to select the photograph that showed the mountains from the doll's perspective. Lack of perspective taking during the pre-operational stage results in what Piaget called *egocentric speech*. Apparently, young children do not really communicate with each other but talk past each other. Only in the next stage will speech become social and takes the perspective of the others into account.

During the third stage of cognitive development, the *concrete-operational stage* that begins at about age seven, the child understands that attributes like number or volume are invariant, and they no longer think egocentrically. However, children's thinking is still fixed in concrete situations. They are not yet able to systematically test a hypothesis that includes two variables. For example, when children had to balance weights on two sides of a scale, they were not able to systematically explore the effects of mass and distance from the center of the scale in order to work out the lever principle. Children are able to test this type of abstract hypotheses at the *formal operational stage* which is the fourth stage beginning at approximately age 12.

There have been various criticisms and extensions of Piaget's theory. Let us first discuss criticisms of Piaget's theory of cognitive development before we review an extension, Kohlberg's theory of moral development.

We look at five different kinds of criticism raised by later researchers, namely (1) the fact that some capacities appear earlier than Piaget thought; (2) reasoning may be domain specific; (3) cognitive development may be reduced to the development of some basic mechanism, such as the amount of information the mind can handle at one point in time; (4) some parts of Piaget's theory may be wrong; or (5) the theory has hidden assumptions that may be wrong.

First, some capacities have been shown to appear much earlier than Piaget thought. Based on whether children search hidden objects, Piaget assumed that children achieve object permanence only toward the end of the second year. However, deciding to search an object might be a more complicated process and thus emerges later than knowing that the object still exists. The challenge for developmental psychologists was to find a different way to examine object permanence. Renée Baillargeon designed a task that did not involve search and hence was much easier for children. It exploited the fact that children look longer at surprising events. Imagine you open your laptop and push the screen completely down until it is on the table. When an object, for example a glass of water, is behind the screen, it is not possible to push it down completely; the screen cannot move through the object. In analogy to the laptop example, the researchers accustomed children to a screen that was completely opened until it was on the table again, which is the process of habituation we have discussed earlier. They then placed a box behind the screen. It was impossible to open the screen completely because the box was in the way. When the experimenter lifted the screen, the box was hidden. Hence, children had to know that the box still existed in order to be surprised when the screen opened completely and apparently moved through the box. Indeed, children looked longer at impossible events where the screen seemed to move through the box than to possible events where the screen stopped up when it hit the box. With this technique, Baillargeon (1987) was able to reveal that some children down to 3½ months showed evidence of object permanence.

Similarly, Piaget assumed that perspective taking in children emerges at the age of about seven to eight years. Yet later studies showed that the three mountains task was too difficult for children; with easier tasks, children down to the age of 3 or 4 were able to take the perspective of others. However, this does not mean that perspec-

tive taking is easy. Even adults have difficulties taking the perspective of others, for example when they have to tell an event they know but others do not know (see Keysar & Barr, 2002). Adult speakers regularly overestimate to what degree listeners understand their message, showing that egocentric thought exists beyond childhood.

Second, Piaget's theory is domain general. It fits well into Fodor's (1983) framework, discussed in Chapter 2, that the mind is composed of specialized senses but that the central part processes information in a domain-general form. According to Fodor and classical theorists in cognitive development, reasoning about all domains is based on the same kind of knowledge structures and develops as a universal capacity.

In Chapter 2, I also mentioned the notion that the mind is composed of domain-specific modules. We have seen that face perception is special. Another potential module is the human capacity for language. A growing number of developmental psychologists have assumed that cognitive development is domain specific and that there are core domains (see Wellman & Gelman, 1992). Through interaction with objects, plants and animals, and other people, children develop separate understanding of basic principles in physics, biology, and psychology. Proponents of the domain-specific approach assume that understanding phenomena in physics, biology, and psychology are different from each other and therefore need different kinds of knowledge structures. These theories focus on domain knowledge but less on cognitive abilities and processes.

A famous account for children's understanding of psychological principles is the research on *theory of mind*, which means that children impute mental states, such as beliefs, memories, and feelings, not only to themselves but also to others. The following experiment illustrates how children develop from egocentric thinking to the assumption that others think with their own mind. Children are told the following story: Maxi's mother comes home from shopping. He helps his mother to stow away the items. In the kitchen are two cupboards: a blue and a green one. Maxi puts the chocolate into the *blue* cupboard and then leaves the house for the playground. His mother uses some of the chocolate for a cake and puts it back into the *green* cupboard. When Maxi comes back home, in which cupboard will he look for the chocolate?

Such stories have become known as *false-belief tasks*, where a person believes in a fact ("chocolate in the blue cupboard"), but as the situation changes ("mother puts chocolate into the green cupboard"), this belief becomes false. Using this task, Wimmer and Perner (1983) observed that none of the 3- to 4-year-olds, 57 percent of the 4- to 6-year-olds, and 86 percent of the 6- to 9-year-olds thought that Maxi would look for the chocolate in the blue cupboard where he put it before he left for the playground. The youngest children in this study could not distinguish between their own knowledge that the chocolate is in the green cupboard and Maxi's false belief because he did not see his mother putting the chocolate into the green cupboard.

Third, more basic processes may account for cognitive development. For example, there is the amount of information that can be processed at one point in time, called processing capacity. An infant's processing capacity is limited but increases with age. Some theorists therefore claimed that the quantitative increase in processing capacity can be mapped onto the four Piagetian stages of cognitive development (see Pascual-Leone, 1987). According to these neo-Piagetian theorists, qualitative changes in the child's reasoning abilities can be explained by the quantitative increase in basic processing capacity.

A fourth form of criticism starts from an observation that partially contradicts Piaget's theory but does not question it. One of the earliest and most prominent critics was the Russian psychologist Lev Vygotsky. Let us come back to the notion of egocentric speech. While Piaget thought that such speech has little significance in itself, Vygotsky maintained that such speech plays a crucial role in the child's planning and communication. Vygotsky noted that when children have to solve a difficult problem, they speak to themselves. They need to speak aloud; interrupting their speech hampers the ability to solve the problem. Egocentric speech decreases with the age of the children. Piaget thought that it just disappears. Vygotsky, by contrast, noted that thinking aloud changes to *inner speech*, which means that the child continues to use language to guide problem-solving but remains mute toward the outside.

A final and fundamental form of criticism starts from hidden premises in Piaget's theory. Piaget assumed that the child's development is driven from an inner impetus, such as curiosity or the pleasures of understanding. Vygotsky contradicted. How do children learn to solve problems? They try themselves, and as soon as they encounter an obstacle, they ask their parents and later their teachers. Children grow up in a culture and learn the knowledge of this culture by communicating with other people – achievements in development can be understood as the product of socialization. That is why Vygotsky's work has become known as the *socio-cultural approach*, which assumes that the social and cultural environment of the child determine development, in contrast to the approach by Piaget and other Western psychologists who consider development as determined by factors within the individual.

Although parts of Piaget's theory have become obsolete, he is a towering figure in psychology who single-handedly built a theory of cognitive development during those decades that were the heydays of psychoanalysis in Europe and behaviorism in America. Piaget's theoretical edifice has stood the test of time – at least the larger framework. There have been additions and revisions, but his main findings on object permanence, the conservation of number and volume, and perspective taking are easy to replicate and still form the cornerstone of any theory of cognitive development. Finally, newer theories built on Piaget's work.

A famous example is Kohlberg's theory of moral development. It includes six stages within three levels. Children at the *pre-conventional level* think about avoiding punishment (Stage 1) and later about their self-interest (Stage 2). Young children are concerned with the consequences of actions for themselves. At the subsequent *conventional level*, children think about social norms (Stage 3) and law and order (Stage 4). The moral standards of these older children no longer depend on punishment and self-interest but are still oriented at external norms and rules. At the *post-conventional level*, morality is derived from general principles a society shares, for example human rights (Stage 5) and universal ethical principles (Stage 6). Adolescents reaching this stage do not see morality as rules imposed from outside but as shared moral principles they agree with.

Kohlberg used moral dilemmas to assess the moral stage of a person. One of these is the famous Heinz dilemma about a man named Heinz whose wife has terminal cancer. An overpriced drug could cure his wife but he does not have enough money; there is no legal way to get the drug. The dilemma consists in whether Heinz should steal the drug and enable his wife to survive or act according to the law and allow his wife to die. To assess a stage of moral development, it is not important whether the participant is for or against stealing the medication but what kind of the justification the participant gives. For example, the answer "Heinz should not steal the drug because he will be caught and put in prison" is a Stage 1 answer that emphasizes the consequences; "Heinz should not steal the drug because it is illegal" is a Stage 4 response related to law and order. Finally, "Heinz should not steal the drug because others might need it as badly, and Heinz would take it away from them" would be a Stage 6 answer invoking universal human values. However, the answer "Life as a fundamental value is more important than the rights of the druggist to make money" also counts as a Stage 6 answer because it refers to a universal human value – as said, it is the kind of justification that counts, not the decision.

Like Piaget's theory of cognitive development, Kohlberg's theory of moral development is a stage theory. Moreover, Kohlberg's theory is based on the assumption that children develop moral reasoning capacities.

However, rule-based reasoning about morality is not the only way to arrive at moral decisions. Another line of research discussed the development of interpersonal emotions as the foundation of moral development, for example the development of *empathy*, which is the ability to understand and share the emotions of others. When feeling empathy, a person sees or understands another's emotional state and responds with a similar affective state on their own (see Eisenberg, 2000). In general, theories on moral emotions assume that children develop emotional responses that guide their moral acts. For example, a girl may see a boy suffer, feel with him, and console him. The development of moral emotions is seen as a result of socialization within a culture. This culture-specific view contrasts with Kohlberg's stage theory that assumes that the development of moral reasoning capacities is universal.

When people explain the young man's aggression at the subway station with the fact that his morality is not sufficiently developed, they could mean two things. According to Kohlberg's theory, the young man's moral reasoning capacities may be underdeveloped. On the other hand, as a result of his upbringing, the young man may lack empathy toward other people's suffering that would help him regulate his aggressive behavior.

EMOTIONAL AND SOCIAL DEVELOPMENT

Sigmund Freud put forward a theory of psychosocial development that included five stages: oral, anal, phallic, latent, and genital. The details of Freud's developmental theory are of historical interest because it lacks scientific evidence, with the exception of the oral stage where children through breastfeeding develop attachment to their mothers. However, Freud introduced many new ideas into psychology that did not survive empirical scrutiny but nevertheless inspired important modern research. One field of research that Freud's work made possible was the theory of attachment.

During and after the Second World War, interest in attachment emerged for three reasons. First, at the beginning of the war, more than 700,000 children were evacuated out of London for the fear of air raids. These children – many in their preschool years – were separated from their parents. Second, during the war, many children became orphans and were admitted to orphanages with minimal resources. Finally, after the war, various hospitals still had strict rules for visiting children, such as twice a week for 1 hour. Some hospitals did not allow visits by parents at all. The reason for the restrictions was the fear by doctors that dangerous infections would spread. Moreover, younger children often were upset when their parents left the hospital, which was stressful for the nursing staff (see van der Horst, 2011).

Although the practice of evacuation out of London led to heated debates between those who cared for the safety of the children and psychiatrists who thought that the practice of separation harmed young children, there was little scientific evidence for the psychological effects of separation. During and right after the Second World War, such evidence emerged from descriptions of children living in hospitals and orphanages by psychoanalyst René Spitz (1945). These children were separated from parents and had minimal contact with staff and minimal stimulation, a condition Spitz termed *hospitalism*. Children in such a condition often developed symptoms like passivity and depression. What was missing was *attachment*, the affectional tie that a person forms with another specific person, such as the mother or another primary caregiver. This "tie binds them together in space and endures over time" (Ainsworth & Bell, 1970, p. 50).

How could attachment be explained? To find an answer, John Bowlby – himself a psychoanalyst – turned to *ethology*. Ethology is the biology of behavior. As briefly mentioned in the discussion on instincts, Konrad Lorenz (1937) showed that goslings follow the first moving object they were exposed to. In nature, this is the mother goose. However, in the laboratory, goslings followed a wooden figure or even Konrad Lorenz himself when these were the first moving objects they saw. Lorenz called this process *imprinting*. Although imprinting does not explain human attachment, Bowlby considered attachment to the mother as an evolved adaptation that provided an advantage for survival, which is in the tradition of ethology. Children not only needed food but also a bond including kindness, comfort, attention, touch, and warmth from the one person they could identify with – most often their mother. Remember that children hear the voice of the mother in the womb and after birth they prefer it to other voices, which creates a very first bond. Despite a good theory, Bowlby's theory of attachment lacked empirical support. Although studies on hospitalism showed what happened if the child could not build a relationship with a mother, it did not show that children actively searched for attachment with a primary caregiver.

First evidence came from animal studies by Harry Harlow (1958). He separated young rhesus monkeys from their biological mothers. In their cage, he provided them with the choice between an artificial surrogate mother consisting of a wire rack that delivered milk and an artificial surrogate mother with a fur surface that did not provide milk. The infant monkey spent most time with the fur model and only went to the wire model when it needed milk. This experiment showed that infant monkeys not only needed food but also physical contact and warmth.

Evidence for attachment in human infants came from studies by Mary Ainsworth. She gathered two kinds of evidence. First, she observed how children interacted with their mothers at home both in Uganda and the United States (see Ainsworth & Bowlby, 1991). Second, she complemented observation with a laboratory study that adhered to a strict protocol (see Ainsworth & Bell, 1970). In essence, the mother entered a laboratory room with the baby. After 3 minutes, a stranger entered, and 3 minutes after that the mother unobtrusively left. The baby was now alone with the stranger until the mother returned after another 3 minutes, when the stranger left. The mother stayed in the room until the baby was at ease and played with toys. Then the mother said "goodbye" and left the baby alone for 3 minutes (this period was shortened if the baby was too distressed and needed comfort) before the stranger came in, again for 3 minutes. Finally, the mother returned. The experimenter observed from an adjacent room the responses of the baby with the mother, the stranger, and while it was alone.

Through observation in the real world and in the laboratory, Ainsworth came to distinguish secure and insecure attachment. Children developed secure attachment during their first year of life if their mothers consistently responded to crying by picking them up. Such children socialized with strangers and explored the environment when the mother was present. They were distressed when the mother left but happy when she returned. Children developed insecure attachment when their mother was emotionally irresponsive during their first year of life. There are two kinds of insecure attachment. Insecure-avoidant children did not show signs of distress when the mother left and avoided proximity to the mother when she returned. Children with an insecure-ambivalent attachment style were often passive in the presence of their mother but highly distressed when the mother left. They were ambivalent when the mother returned.

Based on Ainsworth's research, Bowlby postulated that children develop internal working models, which are beliefs stored in memory about what they have learned in the interaction with their mother. A child whose mother responds to their distress by picking them up or soothing them expects that their mother will do this in the future. A child whose mother does not respond to distress or even responds negatively develops an internal working model that their mother does not respond to their distress. Bowlby argued that children who develop internal working models of insecure attachment may as adults expect that other people do not respond or respond negatively to their needs and feelings. Such expectations may lead to maladaptive behavior in relationships, such as not showing distress or feelings towards a partner. In line with a central tenet of cognitive psychology, it is the expectations about a partner's response and not reality itself that guide interpersonal behavior. However, the expectations stem from experiences with reality. Attachment is not driven from an internal impetus, like in Piaget's or Kohlberg's theory of development. Likewise, Bowlby's theory contradicts psychoanalytic theories that considered early experience of the child as the product of unconscious inner conflicts, not of experience with outer reality. According to Bowlby, one task of psychotherapy consists in revealing maladaptive attachment patterns acquired in childhood in order to learn adaptive interpersonal behavior.

Children who develop insecure attachment may not only have problems with relationships but may also become irresponsive and insensitive parents. However, insecure attachment is not fate but responds quite well to interventions to increase parental sensitivity and children's attachment security (Bakermans-Kranenburg, Van IJzendoorn, & Juffer, 2003).

Healthy attachment in infancy means that a child develops basic trust to a caregiver, which belongs to the first stage of a well-known theory of psychosocial development outlined by Erik Erikson (1994/1959). This theory postulates eight stages, and at each stage, an individual can succeed or fail. Erikson's theory encompasses the whole lifespan, beginning at birth and ending with old age. *Lifespan development* extends standard developmental theories, such as the ones by Freud and Piaget, who considered development from birth to adolescence.

Let us look at four of the eight stages in Erikson's model of psychosocial development. At the first stage, during the first 18 months of life, children will develop trust in their primary caregiver. They may develop distrust if they do not succeed in finding trust – presumably due to lack of affectional ties, as reviewed earlier. At the fifth stage of Erikson's model, adolescents have to find their role in life. Their search for identity may succeed or result in confusion. During the next stage, as young adults, people develop intimacy. Not finding a partner may in the worst case result in isolation. The last stage is old age. When people succeed, they may gain wisdom by accepting life in its fullness, including accomplishments and defeats. People who fail may experience guilt; a feeling of not having accomplished important goals may lead to despair.

Following up Erikson's model of identity development, Robert Havighurst (1974) noted that every person encounters problems he has to solve during the course of life – so-called *developmental tasks*. Developmental tasks arise at certain periods in life and depend on maturation, cultural expectations, and personal characteristics such as personality and ambition. According to Havighurst, success at solving a developmental task leads to happiness in the individual, approval from society, and success in the future. By contrast, failure to solve a developmental task leads to unhappiness, disapproval, and difficulties at solving related future tasks.

Learning to walk or talk are early developmental tasks that depend on maturation. Late in life, hearing impairment and memory loss, illness, or physical decline depends on biological processes, too. Other tasks are specific for a family or self-imposed and therefore not universal, as Erikson's stage theory would postulate. A few owners of traditional family businesses may pose a developmental task to their offspring by expecting them to continue the business in the future. By contrast, the task to establish a new business is often self-imposed; it is a developmental task based on personal ambition. Finally, some developmental tasks depend on cultural norms, such as retirement at a certain age in Western cultures.

SELF-CONTROL: LONG-TERM PREDICTIONS FROM CHILDHOOD TO ADULTHOOD

Developmental psychology describes how mental capacities grow and decline during the lifespan. The question arises whether a capacity in childhood could predict outcomes in adulthood. In the previous section, we mentioned that attachment experiences in childhood affect adult attachment patterns. In this section, we discuss in more detail how self-control in children affects their behavior as adults.

Why do we sometimes eat another piece of chocolate even though we know that too much is unhealthy? One popular answer is that we could not resist temptation. We have a problem of *self-control*. This term is used to denote that a person has to inhibit a spontaneous but harmful impulse. Unhealthy eating is one example. Other temptations include gambling, shopping, or procrastinating by surfing the internet instead of studying. One possible explanation for the young smoker's aggression at the subway station might also be lack of self-control.

Some people can inhibit impulses better than others. This observation gave rise to the question whether the degree of self-control as a child could predict the ability to resist temptations as an adult. A measure of self-control for children that made it into popular culture is the *marshmallow test*, introduced by Walter Mischel in the early 1960s (for an overview, see Mischel, Shoda, & Rodriguez, 1989).

The test measures *delay of gratification*; that is, how long a child can resist an immediate reward to receive a greater reward later. In the classical task, a preschool girl (or boy) sits at a table and sees a marshmallow in front of her. The experimenter tells the child that she has to leave the room but will come back later. If the girl waits with eating the marshmallow, so the instruction of the experimenter, she will get a second one and then can eat both of them; if she eats the marshmallow while the experimenter is outside the room, she will not get the second marshmallow. The experimenter leaves the room and observes through a peephole or a camera whether the child can keep her impulses in check and delay gratification in order to get the desired reward. A more refined measure is the average time children can wait until they eat the marshmallow.

In some situations, inhibition is more difficult than in others. For example, children eat the marshmallow earlier when it is visible on the table than when it is covered and hence invisible. To see a reward increases temptation. Young children do not yet have optimal strategies to prevent temptation. When given the choice how to resist temptation, 4-year-olds choose to see the marshmallow instead of covering it – some think this is a good strategy because it makes them feel good. Only towards the end of age 4 do children seem to realize that this strategy is counterproductive and that they had better cover the marshmallow. Exposing or hiding the marshmallow is a strategy that changes the environment. As they grow older, children may possess or learn strategies related to thinking about the reward in order to resist temptation. For example, they may think "fun thoughts" to distract themselves. By contrast, when they think of the reward during waiting, they have a harder time resisting the temptation even if the reward is hidden. Despite this developmental progress, when the reward is visible and participants in the study are left to their own devices, children of the same age differ in their ability to resist temptation and delay gratification.

Does the ability to resist temptation in early childhood predict abilities of the same individuals later in life? The marshmallow test to examine self-control in preschoolers indeed predicted various abilities in adolescence (see Mischel et al., 1989). When individuals resisted temptation and delayed gratification longer in early childhood, their parents judged them as being competent, intelligent, and better able to concentrate and make plans in adolescence. These adolescents were also better able to delay gratification, tolerate frustration, and pursue goals than their peers who showed less self-control when they were preschoolers. The outcome of the marshmallow test at age 4 not only predicted parent ratings but also scores on the SAT, a standardized test of academic aptitude used in college admissions.

Mischel and his colleagues found that self-control in preschoolers predicted outcomes in *adolescents*. Could self-control in childhood predict outcomes in the lives of *adults*? A research team in Dunedin, New Zealand, explored this question by following over 1,000 people from childhood to adulthood (Moffitt et al., 2011). They measured self-control from age 3 to 11 as reported by trained observers, parents, teachers, and the children themselves about behaviors that indicate self-control, such as frustration, impulsivity, and lack of persistence. **High self-control predicted better health and wealth and less criminal behavior.** Individuals who had low self-control as a child were more likely to develop substance dependence, overweight, and hypertension. These measures are known to predict age-related diseases and premature mortality. Low self-control resulted in outcomes that predict financial problems later in life, such as low income, poor saving habits, and credit problems. People who had low self-control as a child were more likely to be single parents. Finally, low self-control predicted a higher likelihood of a criminal conviction.

The Dunedin study could exclude several alternative explanations and thus strengthen the conclusion that self-control and not some confounding variables (see Box 5.1) predict health, financial outcomes, and criminal activity.

Box 5.1 Confounding variables

It is well-known that *socio-economic status*, which is derived from a person's income, education, and occupation, is closely related to self-control. Hence, parents' socio-economic status, not self-control, might have an effect on their children's income at age 32. It might be, then, that children whose parents have more income, higher education, and a better job possess better self-control at age 3 to 11 and will have a higher income at age 32. In this case, the correlation between self-control in childhood and income at age 32 is caused by a third variable, socio-economic status. The authors used statistical techniques to compute the influence of self-control on income when the influence of socio-economic status is statistically removed (or as statisticians say, "it is controlled for"). If it were the parents' socio-economic status and not their children's self-control that influenced income at age 32, the correlation between self-control and later income would disappear.

Similarly, intelligence is correlated with self-control. Hence, influence of intelligence was statistically removed from the calculation. Again, if intelligence but not self-control accounted for higher income, the correlation between self-control and later income would disappear.

In fact, self-control continued to be correlated with income and all other outcomes even when the influence of socio-economic status and intelligence was statistically removed, supporting the notion that higher self-control in childhood – independently from socio-economic status and intelligence – leads to higher income about 20 years later.

One way low self-control might impair adult outcomes are bad decisions in adolescence that lead to harmful lifestyles whose consequences are difficult to escape. To illustrate, a 15-year-old high school student might begin to smoke, a habit that is difficult to quit and has negative long-term consequences for health; a boy may drop out of school, which diminishes his job prospects; or a teenage girl may become pregnant – the focus on child rearing impairs school performance and diminishes financial prospects. Indeed, the authors showed that adolescent mistakes were predicted by low self-control in childhood. Moreover, statistical analyses suggest that these mistakes contributed to lower income, financial struggles, substance dependence, single-parent child-rearing, and crime.

The interpretation of the findings from the Dunedin study could be questioned because the children grew up in different homes. It is therefore possible that the environment influenced factors that determined both the development of self-control and the outcomes. Although home environment is a potential confounding variable, it cannot be as easily measured and statistically removed as socio-economic status and intelligence do. However, the research team collected a second set of data on dizygotic twins who were reared together. As these twins grew up in the same environment with the same parents, these children had the same socio-economic status and family background. Even intelligence is likely to be more similar than the intelligence of children who are not siblings or reared apart because siblings share some of the genetic setup and share the home environment that contributes to intellectual capacity. For over 500 dizygotic twins from England and Wales, Moffitt et al. (2011) examined the relationship of self-control at age 5 and outcomes 7 years later that were early warning signs of later ill health, financial problems, and criminal behavior. Indeed, the twin who had lower self-control at age 5, compared to his or her sibling, was more likely to begin to smoke, to perform poorly at school, and to show antisocial behavior by age 12.

These results suggest that early interventions to increase self-control might prevent costly mistakes in adolescence that become difficult to amend in adult life. For example, children may learn strategies that make it easier to resist impulses such as gambling, shopping, unprotected sex, and overconsumption of sugar or alcohol.

At the beginning of this section, we noted that children differ in their ability to exert self-control. The results on long-term prediction of self-control on a variety of outcomes suggest that individual differences in personality and intellectual abilities may be quite stable across time.

Recommended literature

Overview

Miller, P.H. (2011). *Theories of developmental psychology* (5th ed.). New York, NY: Worth.

Classical primary sources

Harlow (1958; see references).
Mischel, Shoda, & Rodriguez (1989; see references).
Wimmer & Perner (1983; see references).

6

PERSONALITY AND INTELLIGENCE

Individual differences

The previous chapters described general mechanisms that cause behavior. For example, Liza may have encountered a barking dog as a child – an event that made her fear dogs. However, not every child who hears a barking dog comes to fear them. People differ in their responses to identical situations. That is why psychologists explore individual differences. Where do such differences come from? How can they be measured? And what do they lead to? We first discuss some theories that explain the origin of individual differences before two sections are devoted to the measurement of two kinds of individual differences: personality traits and intelligence. In short, personality psychology examines individual differences in *how* people think, feel, and behave. Why are some people more cautious than others, or more persistent, or more agreeable? Intelligence research, by contrast, examines individual differences in *how well* people can think and deal with their environment. How well can people remember information or solve problems?

In light of the person-situation debate on whether behavior is determined by characteristics of the person or the situation, the question arises to what degree personality predicts behavior. Hence, the final section looks at whether personality traits and intelligence predict life outcomes, such as academic performance, occupational success, health, and longevity.

WHERE DO INDIVIDUAL DIFFERENCES COME FROM?

The idea is old that human beings have a stable character, or personality. Character as used in everyday life or in character education refers not only to attributes of a person but also to her moral excellence. Psychologists therefore prefer the more neutral term *personality*, which denotes patterns of thinking, feeling, and behaving that are characteristic for a person. Yet where do stable personality traits come from? The factors that shape personality are the same as the ones that underlie development. The nature-nurture distinction suggests that personality is either genetically transmitted or stems from the environment – or both. Indeed, personality traits are heritable, but only to a certain degree. According to Rothbart (2007), personality is the product of temperament and experience combined. The term *temperament* refers to general tendencies like positive emotionality or activity level, but also fear or irritability that are assumed to have a biological basis and to be inherited. These tendencies are present in infancy and make up the initial states from which personality develops.

However, genetic factors and therefore temperament can explain only part of an individual's personality. This means that environmental factors contribute to personality traits. Environmental factors may include early childhood experiences. Psychoanalysts thought that unconscious conflicts in early childhood, for example between a forbidden sexual desire and the norms of society, are expressed in adult behavior and preferences. Behaviorists would claim that differences in early learning of response patterns through conditioning may result in behavior differences between adults. The final contributor to personality is socialization. Parents teach their children how to behave within their own culture. For example, self-control in adults is partly the result of early discipline, such as correcting transgressions, which is part of socialization.

Early personality psychologists distinguished among different types of people. This idea has remained popular to this day, maybe because types are intuitively appealing and easy to understand. The most prominent example is the Myers-Briggs Type Indicator (MBTI), which is based on the theory of psychological types by Carl Gustav Jung (2016/1921). Despite its popularity, classification of people into types has its dangers because few people clearly fit one type. There is a continuum between two end points of a scale, for example extraversion and introversion, with most people scoring around the midpoint. By classifying people into types, the MBTI loses information that would make the test more informative. More importantly, it is unknown to what degree the MBTI can predict relevant outcomes such as job performance. For this reason, experts like Pittenger (2005) advise not to use this test in applied settings because there are better instruments available based on the Big Five factor structure, a test that measures personality traits.

THE MEASUREMENT OF PERSONALITY TRAITS

Personality traits are cognitive, emotional, and behavioral characteristics that are stable over time. If such traits predicted personal outcomes, such as behavior or professional success, it would mean that knowing about an individual's personality helps predict his or her behavior and success. We shall see in the last section that personality traits indeed predict a wide array of outcomes; but first, we have to review the basics of personality traits.

Language is rich in trait words. For the English language, Allport and Odbert (1936) counted 17,953 trait words (all adjectives) in an unabridged English dictionary. It would be impracticable to examine all trait words as predictors of thoughts, emotions, and behavior. Fortunately, some trait words are more closely related to one another but not to other trait words. Let us look at 10 of the almost 18,000 trait adjectives: *assertive, energetic, shy, anxious, trusting, cooperative, efficient, orderly, imaginative*, and *artistic*. You may see immediately that the words *assertive* and *energetic* are more closely related to each other than both are related to the other eight words; *shy* and *anxious* are more similar than these two words are to the other eight words. When people have to judge themselves on these trait words, those people scoring high on *assertive* are more likely to score high on *energetic* but not necessarily on *shy* and *anxious*; and those scoring high on *shy* are more likely to score high on *anxious* but not necessarily on *assertive* and *energetic*. A method called factor analysis can be used to determine which trait words group together. Trait words that are more similar constitute (or as statisticians say, "load on") the same factor.

Our list of 10 trait words would yield five factors, with *assertive* and *energetic* loading on the first factor, *shy* and *anxious* on the second,

Table 6.1 How trait words cluster into factors

Factor 1	*Factor 2*	*Factor 3*	*Factor 4*	*Factor 5*
Assertive	Shy	Trusting	Efficient	Imaginative
Energetic	Anxious	Cooperative	Orderly	Artistic

trusting and *cooperative* on the third, *efficient* and *orderly* on the fourth, and *imaginative* and *artistic* on the fifth (see Table 6.1).

Various structures of personality were proposed, including as few as two main factors or as many as 16 personality factors. The most accepted solution today includes five broad factors that describe personality, called the *Big Five* (see Funder, 2013, for a summary). In the example to illustrate factor analysis in Table 6.1, I used 10 trait words that loaded on five factors which make up the "Big Five" factors.

The first factor is *extraversion*, which describes people who are personally warm, sociable, assertive, energetic, adventurous, and enthusiastic. The opposite is *introversion*, that is, people who are less personally warm, sociable, and so forth. They are calmer and more reserved.

The second factor is *neuroticism*. People high in neuroticism tend to be anxious, irritable, depressed, shy, moody, and vulnerable. As this is the only of the five dimensions that is labeled according to its negative end, some theorists proposed to name this factor emotional stability, which describes a person who has a more positive emotional outlook.

The third factor, *agreeableness*, describes individuals who are trusting and forgiving, not demanding, unselfish, cooperative, and modest. The everyday expression "kind" fits this factor well. People who score low on agreeableness tend to be unforgiving, demanding, and selfish.

Fourth, *conscientiousness* means that a person is efficient, orderly, dutiful, achievement-oriented, deliberate, and high in self-discipline. Note how close this last facet of conscientiousness is related to self-control that we discussed in the previous chapter. People who are low in conscientiousness tend to be inefficient, disorderly, impulsive, and lazy.

Fifth, individuals high in *openness* are curious, imaginative, artistic, excitable, and unconventional. They have wide interests. People low on openness score lower on these traits.

Note that the Big Five factors do not constitute a typology – most personality psychologists are not interested in whether a person is best described as extravert, neurotic, agreeable, conscientious, or open but in examining to what degree each of the traits is manifest in one and the same person – to what degree she is extravert, emotionally stable, agreeable, conscientious, and open.

The construction of the Big Five factors is special in another way. Usually, scientists first build a theory and then test it. For example, Jung (2016/1921) postulated his four types before others gathered evidence. In contrast, the five-factor model was not first proposed by a theorist and then tested, like Jung's typology, but it was explored using a bottom-up approach: first the data, then the theory. We have seen that psychologists first collected trait words (Allport & Odbert, 1936). Then people responded on tests that used subsets of these trait words. By means of factor analysis, researchers found the five factors extracted from the responses to the tests. As there had been no theory in the case of the Big Five, the question arose: where do the five factors come from?

We have seen that there are two main causes of personality traits: genes and environment. According to a genetic account, traits may have evolutionary roots because stable dispositions to think, feel, and behave may enable people to adapt to their environment. For example, being kind may help people establish and maintain social relationships. In this case, we would expect that personality traits are universal and that there are no cultural differences. By contrast, cultural accounts of personality assume that the various cultures transmit their norms and mindsets that determine personality. As cultures differ in their norms, mindsets, and educational practices, we may expect different structures of personality across cultures. However, there is evidence for cross-cultural agreement in the Big Five factors; they differ only in details. This finding supports the evolutionary explanation that tasks for survival and adaptation to the environment are the same across cultures. The universality of survival tasks results in the universal structure of personality (see John & Srivastava, 1999).

So far this is the theory of the Big Five factors; yet how do we measure personality traits? One of the tests is the Big Five Inventory (BFI-2; Soto & John, 2017). It begins with "I see myself as someone who . . ." and then lists 60 brief statements that contain trait words, such as "is talkative," "is relaxed, handles stress well," and "worries a lot." Test-takers have to respond on a scale from 1 ("disagree strongly") to 5 ("agree strongly"). Such tests need to be reliable and valid (Box 6.1).

Box 6.1 Reliability and validity

A measure must be reliable, which means that multiple measurements of the same trait provide researchers with virtually the same result. Testers may assess the stability of multiple measurements across time (*test-retest reliability*), across testers (*inter-rater reliability*), and across items within a test (*internal consistency*).

We may deliver the same test twice at an interval of several weeks and assess the stability of the results, which is the *test-retest reliability*. Respondents who scored high on the test some weeks ago should score high again; respondents with low scores should score low again. If there is no correlation or a low correlation between the first and the second tests, the measurement is not reliable. Low test-retest reliability could mean that the dimension we measure is a fleeting state instead of a stable trait. For example, if we ask people "How frustrated are you," it might be that people's frustration changes from day to day and from situation to situation.

Besides test-retest reliability, a measurement scale has to be consistent across testers, which results in high *inter-rater reliability*. When two testers administer the test, the results should be comparable. Tests with low inter-rater reliability lack objectivity.

Internal consistency, the final measure of reliability, means that the items of a scale have to correlate with the scale as a whole. When we measure conscientiousness with 12 items, each individual item should contribute to the measurement of conscientiousness.

Besides reliability, the measure has to be valid. High *construct validity* for an assessment of conscientiousness means that the measure indeed measures conscientiousness and nothing else. To this purpose, *content validity* is important. As we have seen, conscientious people are efficient, orderly, dutiful, hardworking or at least not lazy, achievement oriented, and deliberative. To measure the whole scope of conscientiousness, the items need to cover not only one facet (for example, orderly), but all of them. However, it is also important that the scale does not measure facets unrelated to conscientiousness, such as assertiveness or kindness.

Finally, you want a measure such as conscientiousness to predict important outcomes, such as school or job performance. Such prediction will never be perfect. However, the more our conscientiousness scale correlates to relevant outcomes, the better it predicts them, which is its *predictive validity*.

We said that astrology has no scientific basis. To be more precise, horoscopes may have high test-retest reliability and inter-rater reliability but they lack both content validity and predictive validity; they can neither measure personality nor predict relevant outcomes such as job success.

The Big Five Inventory is a highly reliable test. We shall see that it also has good predictive validity. Moreover, researchers found the same five-factor structure whether they measured the personality traits of a person by self-ratings, ratings by peers, or ratings by teachers. This observation adds support to the notion that the Big Five personality structure is stable across situations and independent of who is judging a person.

Do personality traits remain stable across the lifespan? This question could be understood in two ways. First, are individual differences stable across the lifespan? If Alf is more extraverted than Susy at the age of 14, will he be more likely to be extraverted than Susy at the ages of 25 and 60? Research suggests that the answer is yes. Individual differences tend to be stable across the lifespan, which is called *rank-order stability*. Although individual differences in personality remain stable across the lifespan, rank-order stability increases with age. In other words, personality is more likely to undergo changes in childhood than in young adulthood, and more likely to change in young adulthood than between 50 and 70.

The other way to understand the question about stability has to do with personality development of an individual person. Does Alf change in the extent to which he is extraverted? Does Susy change in the extent to which she is conscientious? The stability of the average level of traits across the lifespan is called *mean-level stability*.

Based on over one million respondents from an online study, Soto, John, Gosling, and Potter (2011) extracted age and gender effects for each of the Big Five personality dimensions. The sample in this cross-sectional study had an age range from 10 to 65.

The trends are depicted in Figure 6.1. There seem to be three relevant age periods; the first from childhood to adolescence (age 10 to about 15); the second from adolescence to early adulthood (15 to about 20); and the third from early adulthood to later adulthood (20 to 65).

Extraversion declines from childhood to adolescence and then remains stable through adolescence and adulthood. Neuroticism is not different for boys and girls at the age of 10. From childhood to adolescence, neuroticism goes up for girls and then declines from adolescence through adulthood. For boys, neuroticism remains stable through early adulthood and declines from middle to later adulthood. The patterns for agreeableness and conscientiousness look quite similar to each other; both decline from childhood to adolescence but increase steeply in adolescence and then increase less steeply through adulthood. Also, openness declines from childhood to adolescence. In adolescence, there is a gender difference where girls show a further decrease but boys remain at about the same level. Openness increases through adult life for both women and men.

Figure 6.1 also shows marked gender differences, especially in adulthood. Women are higher in extraversion, neuroticism, agreeableness, and conscientiousness whereas men are higher in openness. One explanation is that such gender differences emerged during the course of human evolution. For example, a woman might have been more likely to find a mate and therefore to have offspring that carried her genes to the next generation when she was agreeable, whereas a man might have a higher chance of supporting his offspring when he was less anxious. An alternative explanation for these gender differences has been offered by *social role theory*. Each society expects women and men to behave in certain ways. As women in traditional societies have a caring role whereas men have the role as the breadwinner for the family, personality differences might be due to social roles. As a caring wife and mother, a woman is expected to be kind, unselfish, and modest – that is, high on agreeableness. A man, by contrast, is supposed to earn a living to support the family. As anxious men presumably earn less, it would be an advantage to be courageous, that is, low on anxiety which is a facet of the neuroticism scale.

However, there is evidence that neither evolutionary accounts nor social role theory can account for the gender differences found in

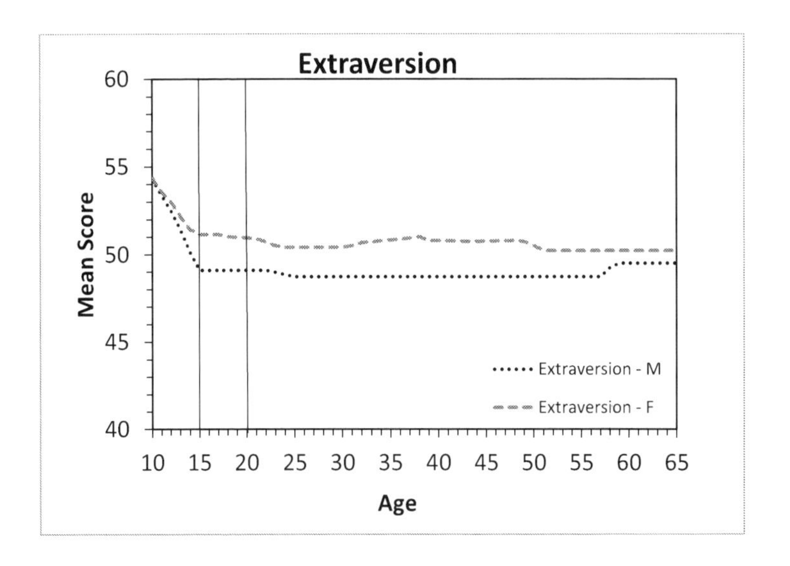

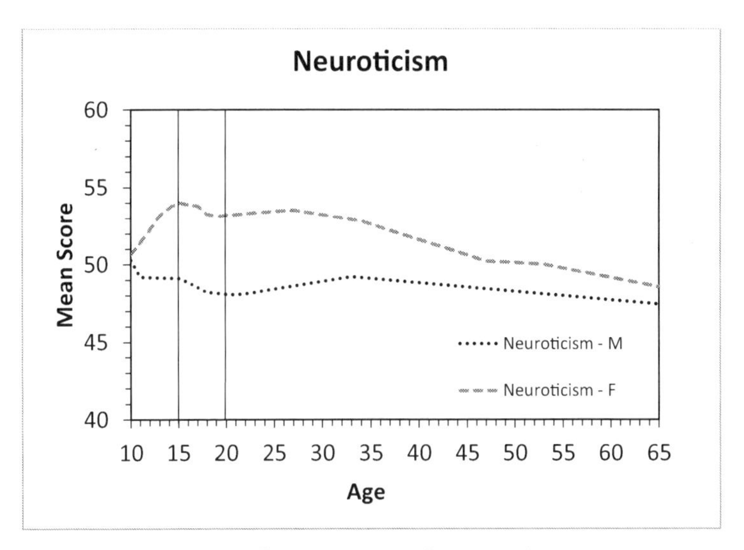

Figure 6.1 Age and gender differences in the big five personality traits
Source: Simplified to show main trends derived from original data by Soto et al. (2011).

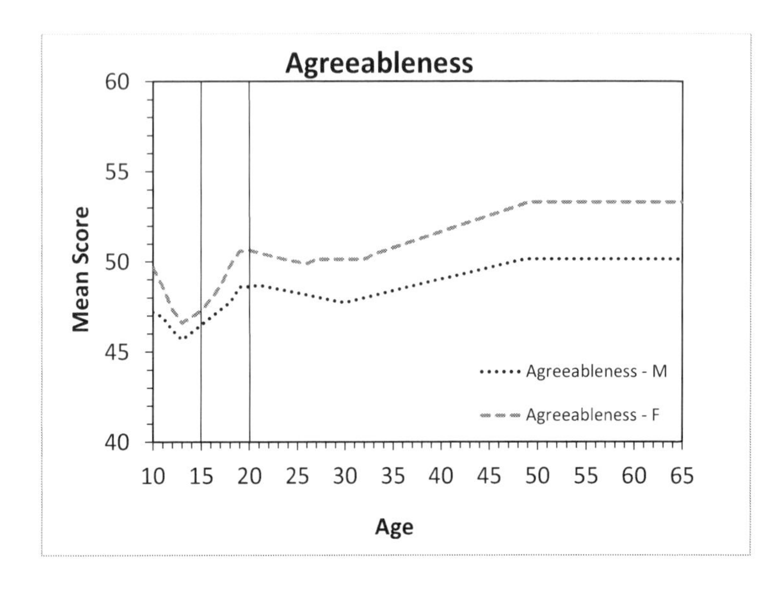

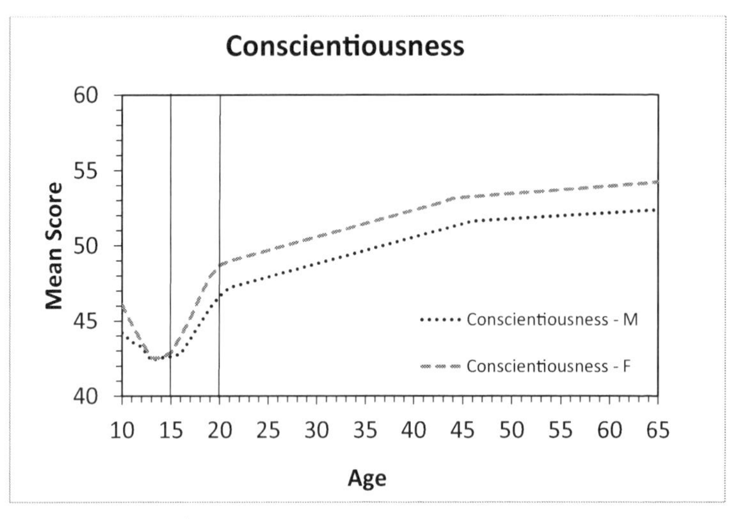

Figure 6.1 Continued

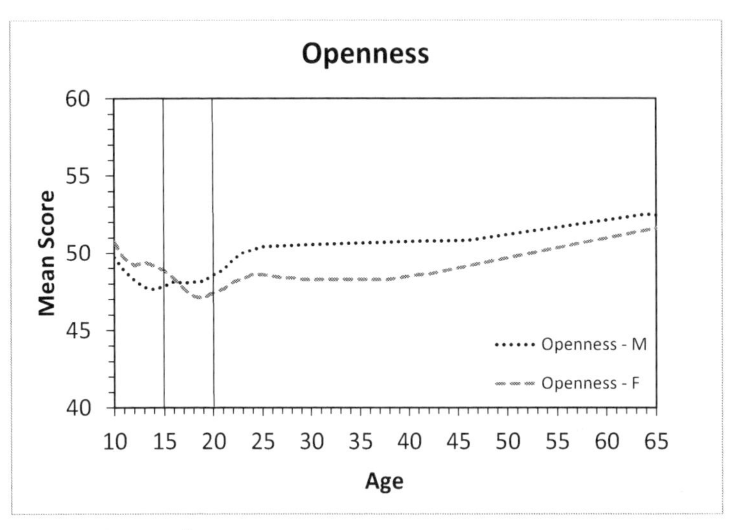

Figure 6.1 Continued

personality traits (see Costa, Terracciano, & McCrae, 2001). According to evolutionary accounts, gender differences should be universal and therefore about the same across cultures, which is not the case. Social role theory, by contrast, would predict that gender differences in traits are smaller in modern, more gender-equal societies. When women and men are equally expected to be caring and to be breadwinners, these personality differences should be smaller in Western countries than in traditional societies. However, Costa et al. found the opposite relationship – that is, gender differences in the Big Five factors were more pronounced in more gender-equal societies in Europe and the United States than in societies with more traditional gender role expectations.

To summarize, we have reviewed the characteristics and measurement of the Big Five personality factors, their development across the lifespan, and gender and cultural differences.

What can personality psychology tell us about the personality of a criminal, Liza's fear of dogs, or George's learning difficulties? Maybe a personality test finds that a person who commits crimes, such as the young smoker in the subway station, is low on conscientiousness, in line with findings that lack of self-control predicts criminal behavior (see previous chapter); Liza may score high on neuroticism. Note that we should not state that Liza (but not other people) fears dogs because she is high on neuroticism but at the same time infer that she is high on neuroticism because she is afraid of dogs. This would be a circular definition. We therefore have to measure neuroticism independently of the observed fear of dogs. There are many possible explanations for George's low school performance, one of them in terms of personality. He might be lazy, which would show as a low score on conscientiousness. However, there is another possibility: George might not be intelligent enough.

INTELLIGENCE

When George performs poorly at school, what does it mean to say that he is not intelligent enough? As a first approximation, we may state that his intellectual capacities are not sufficiently adapted to what is required to function well in his society because *intelligence* is defined as

> *the aggregate or global capacity of the individual to act purposefully, to think rationally and to deal effectively with his environment.* It is global because it characterizes the individual's behavior as a whole; it is an aggregate because it is composed of elements or abilities which, though not entirely independent, are qualitatively differentiable
>
> (Wechsler, 1944, p. 3; italics in the original; for a more detailed overview on intelligence, see Holt et al., 2015, Chapter 10)

The first intelligence test was developed by French psychologist Alfred Binet at the beginning of the 20th century. He wanted to assess children's mental capabilities as early as possible to detect intellectual deficiencies and refer them to special education. To assess the intelligence of children, he gave them tasks adapted to their age. Based on observations, a 4-year-old child was supposed to solve the task, "In daytime it is light; at night it is . . ."; a 6-year-old child, "A centimeter is short, a kilometer is . . ."; and a 9-year-old child, "If you buy chocolate at 4 centimes and you pay 10 centimes, how much change will you get?" If a 6-year-old girl could solve the task of a 9-year-old child, she had (according to Binet) a mental age of 9 years despite her chronological age of 6 years.

After Binet developed his scales and determined mental age of children, German psychologist William Stern introduced the concept of the intelligence quotient (IQ), calculated as the quotient of mental age divided by chronological age multiplied by 100. If an 8-year-old child could solve the tasks of a 10-year-old, the child's IQ is 10 divided by 8 times 100, which yields 125. If, by contrast, a 10-year-old child could solve tasks that corresponded to a mental age of 8, the IQ would be 8 divided by 10 times 100, which yields 80. Later, the concept of mental age was abandoned because it is not suited to calculate the IQ of adults. If a 20-year-old adult could solve tasks that a 60-year-old person could solve, the IQ would be 300! Nowadays intelligence tests are standardized.

Examples of standardized intelligence tests are the *Stanford-Binet test*, derived from the Binet scales, and the *Wechsler Adult Intelligence Scale* (WAIS), developed by David Wechsler in the late 1930s. For standardization, a representative sample of the population – hundreds of respondents – completes the intelligence test. The mean performance is defined as IQ = 100, and one standard deviation is 15 points. Standard deviation is a measure of the spread around a mean. Importantly for the present purpose, 68 percent of a population falls within one standard deviation from the mean. This means that 68 percent of the population has an IQ between 85 and 115. Likewise, around 95 percent of the population has an IQ between 70 and 130. Note that this definition of IQ is not a natural law but a convention. After some time, intelligence tests needed new standardization because average intelligence increased in the last decades, as we discuss later.

Early in the 20th century, psychologists began to address the question how people differ in their mental abilities. Charles Spearman claimed that there is only one *general factor* that makes up intelligence; he called this factor *g*; nowadays it is often referred to as *general mental ability*. He derived this conclusion from the fact that all test scores are correlated to each other, which suggests that a person who does well on one test also does well on all the others. Soon critics noted that although all tests are moderately correlated to each other, there are several clusters of highly correlated tests, and intelligence researchers began to develop tests under the assumption that intelligence includes more than one factor. The most prominent multifactor solution came from Louis Leon Thurstone (1938), who found seven factors and proposed seven primary mental abilities, including perceptual speed, spatial visualization, number facility, word fluency, verbal comprehension, associative memory, and reasoning.

A compromise between the general factor assumption and Thurstone's multiple factor solution has been a widely recognized division of general intelligence into two factors: fluid intelligence and crystallized intelligence. *Fluid intelligence* is the aptitude to solve problems where no ready-made strategies exist. Inductive reasoning – the kind of generalization from singular instances discussed in Chapter 2 (Wason, 1960) – and creativity are supposed to belong to fluid intelligence. *Crystallized intelligence*, by contrast, is the aptitude to apply prior knowledge to problems, such as learning and using vocabulary or using knowledge about problem-solving strategies. Three pieces of evidence support the division into fluid and crystallized intelligence (see Nisbett, 2009). First, as mentioned in Chapter 4, brain lesions in the frontal lobe result in deficiencies in executive function. Such lesions reduce scores on fluid intelligence but not on crystallized intelligence. On the other hand, people suffering from autism show the reverse pattern: high fluid but low crystallized intelligence. This is a double dissociation that shows that there are two different systems or mechanisms underlying fluid and crystallized intelligence. Second, brain imaging studies revealed that tasks that tap fluid intelligence and tasks that tap crystallized intelligence activate different areas of the brain. Finally, there is a pronounced difference in the lifespan trajectory of the two kinds of intelligence. While fluid intelligence increases until the mid-twenties and then declines, crystallized intelligence increases with age and then flattens but does not decrease, even in old age.

The most frequently used intelligence test, the WAIS, is based on the assumption that there are four different mental abilities. The current version, WAIS-IV, has four scales to assess verbal comprehension, working memory, perceptual reasoning, and processing speed.

One problem with traditional intelligence tests such as Stanford-Binet and WAIS is that they rely on tasks that depend on schooling. For example, verbal comprehension, one scale of the WAIS, is something children train at school. These tests seem to measure *achievement* (actual performance of an individual on a task, often as a result of training) instead of *aptitude*, which is the intellectual potential to perform tasks.

Moreover, tests such as the WAIS are culture dependent. People from non-Western cultures or with little schooling may be at a disadvantage when taking the test. It is therefore the aim of test makers to create intelligence assessments that are culture-fair. The most famous such test is Raven's matrices (see Figure 6.2). As you can see, the test does not include written materials and can therefore be

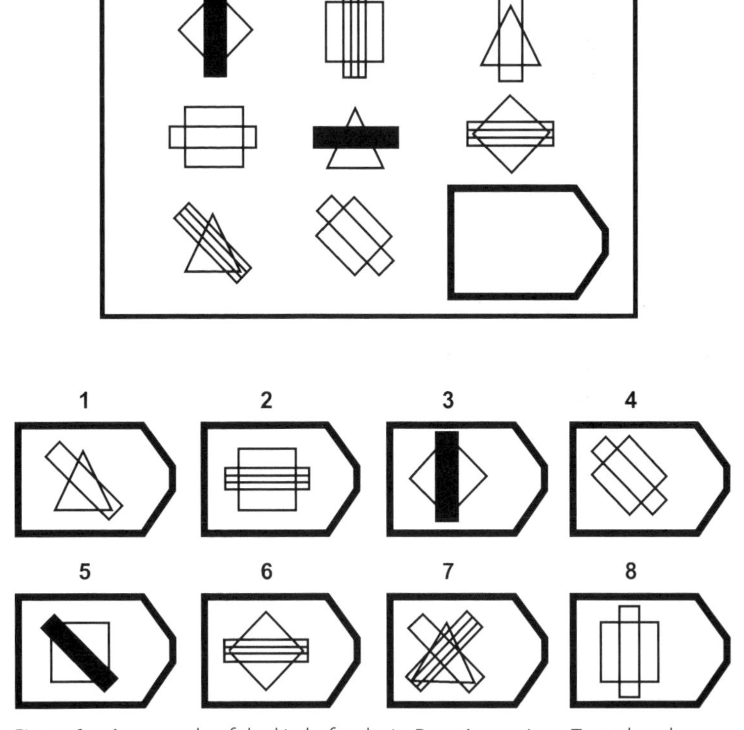

Figure 6.2 An example of the kind of tasks in Raven's matrices. Test-takers have to choose from the eight options in the bottom half the one that fits to complete the panel in the top half. Here, option #5 is the correct one. Note that test publishers do not allow copying exact tasks; hence, this is an example from an article that used similar tasks using the same principle.

Source: Carpenter, P. A., Just, M. A., & Shell, P. (1990, p. 407).

solved by any person, even if they never have learned to read. However, some scientists doubt that Raven's matrices are indeed culture-fair, as we shall see later.

Another way to construct culture-fair tests would consist in assessing what aptitudes are necessary or valued in a particular culture and then construct the intelligence test according to these culture-specific aptitudes. This strategy has been thought through in theory but rarely implemented in testing.

Although intelligence is to some degree heritable, environmental and cultural factors, especially schooling, play an important role. One consequence of environmental and cultural influences on intelligence is the Flynn effect. This effect was named after intelligence researcher James Flynn who discovered that since around the 1930s, intelligence scores increased by about 3 points per decade in the West (e.g., Flynn, 1987). As intelligence tests are standardized at regular intervals, such that the average IQ is 100 and one standard deviation is 15 IQ points, a person with average intelligence in 1960 had an IQ of 100 and a person with average intelligence in 2010 would also have an IQ of 100. However, these values are based on different standards. Given the observation that IQ increased about 3 points per decade, we can compute that an adult who had an IQ of 100 in 2010 would according to the standards in 1960 have had an IQ of 115. On the other hand, the person who had an IQ of 100 in 1960 would have had an IQ of 85 in 2010.

What causes the Flynn effect? One reason is improved diet. For example, adding multivitamins and iodine increases IQ in children with deficiencies in these nutrients (Protzko, 2017). However, nutrition would explain only part of the Flynn effect in Western countries; since World War II, few children have suffered from lack of nutrients.

An important factor is schooling and the shift from menial and industrial jobs to a knowledge economy where exactly those skills count that are measured by intelligence tests. We noted earlier that there is some doubt that Raven's matrices are a culture-fair intelligence test. The most important reason for this doubt is the considerable increase in scores on Raven's matrices during the last decades, even more than the scores on culture-dependent tests like the WAIS (Trahan, Stuebing, Hiscock, & Fletcher, 2014). Presumably schooling in the Western hemisphere shifted from rote learning to pattern recognition and abstract reasoning, which are skills measured by Raven's matrices.

Finally, parents have fewer offspring but invest more time and resources in the few children they have. Actually, in some Western countries, the Flynn effect flattened but it is likely to occur in developing countries where there is ample room for improvement in the form of diet, schooling, jobs that need intellectual skills, and reduction in family size, with concomitant growth in parental investment for each child.

Our discussion of reasons for the Flynn effect helps resolve one of the most heated debates in psychology. The debate revolved around the observation that there were small but reliable differences in intelligence scores between white and black test-takers. The interpretation that this difference expresses genetic differences in intellectual aptitude has to be made with caution because it may lead to discriminatory policies. For example, when differences in intelligence are inherited, why should the state provide special education programs to promote intelligence for those with low intelligence scores? However, the proven effects of schooling on intelligence suggest that the differences in intelligence scores between races may be caused by cultural and social class differences. The fact that there are genetic differences in intellectual abilities and race differences in intelligence scores does not necessarily mean that race differences have to be genetic and fixed. In fact, genes account for roughly half of the variation in intelligence scores, the other half being determined by environment. This means that race differences in intelligence scores might be accounted for by schooling. Race differences in intelligence and their potential policy implications have been a prime example on how carefully scientists should interpret research data.

INDIVIDUAL DIFFERENCES IN PRACTICE

In the previous chapter we saw that a simple test of delay of gratification in children can predict outcomes like school performance, health, substance abuse, and criminal convictions later in life. Some employers use intelligence and personality tests to assess job applicants under the assumption that these tests help select the best candidates. Do such tests indeed predict academic and job success? Moreover, do intelligence and personality tests also predict health in the same way that self-control in childhood predicts health outcomes? Let us look at academic and job success first and then at health outcomes.

Many colleges require entry tests, such as the SAT. Although such tests are supposed to assess academic aptitude, they are so closely correlated to intelligence tests that some researchers offered equations to convert SAT scores into IQ scores. As the scores of the SAT and other academic and vocational entry tests are widely available, researchers often use such assessments as a measure for general mental ability (the *g* factor discussed in the previous section).

The correlations between IQ scores and academic performance are more than 0.5 for high school students and around 0.4 in college students (Kuncel, Hezlett, & Ones, 2004). Box 6.2 illustrates what a correlation coefficient of 0.4 means. However, these correlations did not consider confounding variables, such as socio-economic status. Students from higher socio-economic backgrounds tend to attend better schools and schooling influences intelligence, which leads to better academic performance at high school and college. Yet it is certain that intelligence explains academic performance above and beyond socio-economic status.

Similarly, intelligence predicts job performance quite well, with correlation coefficients from various meta-analyses converging at around 0.5 (Kuncel & Hezlett, 2010). Interestingly, general mental ability predicts job performance as well as specific aptitudes tailored to the job do, and better than job experience or personality traits (Schmidt & Hunter, 2004). The observation that intelligence predicts both academic and job performance does away with the popular myth that intelligence and academic success are useless for work life. If this had been the case, intelligence would not predict job performance.

Finally, the more complex the job is, the better intelligence predicts job performance (see Kuncel & Hezlett, 2010). As a consequence, an intelligent person also earns more money than his or her less intelligent brother or sister (Murray, 2002). Remember the study by Moffitt et al. (2011): by comparing siblings who were reared together, researchers can neglect parents' socio-economic status as confounding variable. Moreover, siblings are more similar than unrelated individuals when it comes to both genetic predispositions and home environment, further suggesting that intelligence influences life outcomes.

Box 6.2 What does a correlation of $r = 0.4$ mean?

In Box 3.1, we reviewed the correlation coefficient and discussed that correlation is not causation. We have now seen that the correlation between intelligence and high school performance is around 0.4. How could we explain such a number to a layperson? For the sake of simplicity, let us assume that intelligence is either high or low and academic performance is either good or poor. Such a correlation can be depicted with the following frequencies (see Table 6.2; see Rosenthal & Rubin, 1982; Funder, 2013).

Table 6.2 Depiction of the correlation $r = 0.4$ with frequencies

		Intelligence		
		High	*Low*	*Total*
School performance	Good	70	30	100
	Poor	30	70	100
Total		100	100	200

We assume that there are 100 students with high intelligence and 100 students with low intelligence. Likewise, 100 students perform well and 100 poorly. When the correlation is 0.4, the difference between high and low equals 40, that is, 0.4 times 100. In order to arrive at the accurate numbers, you have to multiply the correlation coefficient by 100; then add and subtract 20, that is, half of 40, from 50, which is half of the total in each column or row. Adding 20 to 50 yields 70 and subtracting 20 from 50 yields 30, as depicted in the table. Some basic arithmetic is sufficient to derive frequencies from correlations (for the mathematical derivation of this depiction of correlation coefficients, see Rosenthal & Rubin, 1982). In conclusion, of the 100 highly intelligent students, 70 perform well and 30 poorly; of the 100 students with low intelligence, 30 perform well and 70 perform poorly. A correlation of 0.4 means that the prediction accuracy is 70 percent; this is quite considerable.

Likewise, a smaller correlation of 0.1 means prediction accuracy of 55 percent (Table 6.3).

Table 6.3 Depiction of the correlation $r = 0.1$ with frequencies

		Intelligence		
		High	Low	Total
School performance	Good	55	45	100
	Poor	45	55	100
Total		100	100	200

Even a small correlation of 0.03 predicts an outcome with an accuracy of 58.5 percent. This may seem unimpressive, but some well-known medications are no more effective than that. For example, taking aspirin reduces the incidence of heart attacks, but the correlation is a low 0.03. However, this minuscule association meant that there were 85 fewer heart attacks among the more than 22,000 patients who took aspirin (Rosenthal, 1990). With large numbers, even small correlations may have big effects.

Intelligence is not the only predictor of school and work performance. Remember that better self-control at the age of 4 predicted higher SAT scores (Mischel et al., 1989). Similarly, grit – which is a combination of persistence and passion and is related to self-control and conscientiousness – predicted academic success above and beyond intelligence (Duckworth, Peterson, Matthews, & Kelly, 2007). Hence, it seems that a combination of intelligence, persistence, and passion best predict academic and job performance. Presumably, intelligence tests predict how well a person can cope with any job, whereas personality traits predict how well a person fits to a specific job.

Personality and intelligence tests do not only predict academic and occupational success but also health outcomes. Let us look at personality first. Common sense says that optimism and good humor are healthy; many self-help books recommend fostering optimism to prevent or cure disease. If you ask people about their health, research reveals that there is a positive correlation between optimism and self-reported health, but such findings cannot be confirmed if one takes objective measures of health, such as longevity, which is the most reliable measure. It seems that optimists judge themselves to be healthier without really being so (see Friedman & Kern, 2014). One reason for this lack of relationship between happiness and health has to do with the fact that not every activity that makes people happy may promote good health. For example, watching sports on TV, drinking beer, and eating lots of sweets may make people happy in the short term but does not promote health in the long term. On the other hand, living in a stable marriage and daily walks in nature may make people happy and also promote health. In other words, it is not happiness in itself that influences health but activities that either promote or impair health.

The one factor that reliably increases objective health is conscientiousness, one of the "Big Five" traits. Indeed, childhood conscientiousness predicts longevity decades later. How can such a finding be explained? Friedman and Kern (2014) list several effects of conscientiousness having positive health outcomes. First, conscientious individuals engage in healthier behaviors – they tend to smoke less, eat healthier food, and use seat belts. These observations are in line with the findings reviewed in the previous chapter that self-control improves health (Moffitt et al., 2011). Second, conscientious people are more likely to have stable marriages and select healthier environments. Third, as we have already seen, conscientious individuals have more success at school and in their jobs. As they earn more, they can buy healthier food and pay for superior health services. Even in case a career falters, conscientious people are better prepared to take compensatory action that alleviates the detrimental effects of a professional setback.

Intelligence tests also predict longevity; intelligent people live longer. Why might intelligence lead to higher longevity? Hauser and Palloni (2011) suggest that intelligent people develop health-related attitudes and behaviors that result in longer lives. It is even possible that high mental ability increases life duration because intelligent people are good patients. A "good patient" is able to learn about the disease and its best treatment, to reason, and to solve problems. Intelligent patients are better able to master these tasks and therefore live longer (Gottfredson, 2004). However, a study with more than 10,000 high school graduates showed that rank in class was a better predictor of longevity than was IQ (Hauser & Palloni, 2011). As rank within class depends not only on intelligence but even more on non-intellectual factors such as conscientiousness, it seems that personality – mainly conscientiousness – predicts longevity better than intelligence. To conclude, intelligence predicts longevity but conscientiousness predicts longevity even better.

In sum, individual differences in stable characteristics, such as personality traits and intelligence, predict important personal outcomes. Personality psychologists have used such findings to argue for the predictive power of personality factors in the person-situation debate mentioned in the introduction. Yet some behaviors are difficult to predict by measures of individual differences. We are going to see in the next chapter that behaviors like obedience or helping are better explained by situational factors.

Recommended literature

Overview

Funder (2013; see references).

Important primary sources

Flynn (1987; see references).
Soto et al. (2011; see references).

7

LIVING WITH OTHERS

Social psychology

By looking at stable dispositions within a person to explain behavior, the previous chapter shed light on the person side of the person-situation debate. When we looked at the young smoker's attack on the subway employee, we looked at his personality. Another approach considers the situation side of the person-situation debate by asking what triggered the young man's aggression. In general, social psychology explores the processes of social interactions and their origins in the situation.

We begin with two classical studies that demonstrate how scientists can transfer real-world situations – obedience to authority and helping – into the laboratory. These studies show the power of the situation. The subsequent section on social cognition reveals that it is not the situation itself but its interpretation that determines a person's perception, judgment, and behavior toward another person. The last two sections pertain to human mate attraction and living in groups.

THE POWER OF SITUATION: TWO CLASSICAL STUDIES

Some behaviors are puzzling. How could so many ordinary Germans get involved in the Holocaust? Or why do people sometimes not help – even by simply calling the police – when a victim is attacked and needs help? In fact, these observations are hard to explain with stable personality dispositions, and social psychologists began to explore situational factors to explain such behavior. We are going to look at two classical studies that demonstrate the power of the situation.

Obedience to authority

In the early 1960s, philosopher Hannah Arendt followed the trial of Adolf Eichmann, one of the highest-ranking organizers of the Holocaust. From this trial and other materials Arendt concluded that officers and soldiers who committed the crimes were not sadists; they were normal citizens who became murderers within a murderous system. Arendt spoke of the "banality of evil."

Stanley Milgram, a psychologist at Yale University, wondered whether the banality of evil could be demonstrated with average American citizens. To this purpose, he set up an experiment where a participant in the experiment was told that he had to play the role of a "teacher" who had to punish a "student" with electric shocks whenever the student made a mistake in a word learning task. The experimenter would tell the participant when to punish the student, who in fact was a confederate of the experimenter and did not receive real shocks. The student had to solve a memory task and at every mistake the experimenter instructed the participant to administer a shock. Before the experiment, the participant received a shock of 45 volts, which is quite painful, but harmless. The first shock was at 15 volts but shock intensity increased by steps of 15 volts, up to 450 volts. The voltages were labeled, ranging from "Slight Shock" at the lower end to "Danger: Severe Shock" at the upper end. When the participant doubted whether he should continue, the experimenter insisted that he continue. At 75 volts, the student began to grunt and moan; at 180 volts, he screamed that he could no longer stand the pain; at 300 volts, the student no longer provided answers and insisted that he is no longer taking part in this experiment and must be released. How far would the participant go? In fact, all participants went up to 300 volts, and 60 percent went up to the maximum intensity, 450 volts.

Milgram concluded that his experiment provided empirical support for Arendt's notion of the "banality of evil." Average citizens are willing to commit atrocities when pressed by an authority.

These findings were so incredible that some skeptics asked whether the participants could have noticed that the "students" did not receive real shocks and just simulated pain. However, when Milgram asked the participants after the experiment to rate how painful the shocks were for the student, they usually answered within the part of the scale that indicated "extremely painful." Moreover, participants showed real signs of distress during the study. In some participants, the signs of distress were severe. The experiment sparked a debate about research ethics (see Box 1.1). Nowadays, psychologists no longer perform such experiments.

We can learn another lesson from the Milgram experiment. Note that Milgram did not ask the participants to administer a shock of 450 volts at once. He used what is called the *foot-in-the-door technique*. The punishment began with a shock of 15 volts and shock intensity increased by steps of 15 volts. Once a person begins to administer shocks, it becomes difficult to say no to deliver the next shock. The foot-in-the-door technique was also used by the Nazis when they trained soldiers as guardians of concentration camps. When a soldier arrived, he was not immediately placed inside the camp. He was first placed on guard outside the camp, then came closer to the prisoners step by step and received more violent assignments. The Milgram experiment models the habituation of guardians to violence quite well.

We encounter the foot-in-the-door technique in everyday life when neighbors want us to help them out with money. They do not begin with a request of £100 but with a small amount, such as £5. The next week, they ask for £10, then £20, £50, and finally £100. When we help them and lend them £5, it is difficult to say no at the next request.

Helping behavior

In 1964 Kitty Genovese, a young waitress, was raped and murdered outside an apartment block when she was on her way home at night. Although dozens of tenants heard Genovese scream, nobody called the police or helped otherwise during the more than 40 minutes the crime lasted. The apathy of average citizens towards a young woman in need of help was appalling. How could such behavior be explained? Two psychologists, John Darley and Bibb Latané (1968), constructed and tested a model of helping behavior that uncovered psychological reasons for the apathy of the residents.

To help in an emergency situation, a person first has to recognize the emergency and then to decide whether she is the person who is responsible to help.

Two mechanisms prevent people from recognizing a situation as an emergency: observational learning and pluralistic ignorance. We encountered observational learning in Chapter 1. In the same way people may learn from others to be aggressive, they may learn from others to help. For example, after drivers see someone help a woman standing by a car with a flat tire, they are more likely to help when they see another, similar situation some miles later. In this situation, observational learning leads to positive outcomes.

In ambiguous situations, by contrast, pluralistic ignorance may emerge. When a man lies at the wayside, it is often unclear whether he fainted and needs help or is drunk and is sleeping. Margaret may think in private that it could be an emergency, but she sees that other bystanders do not react. As everybody seems to think it is not an emergency, she thinks this as well. *Pluralistic ignorance* emerges if all bystanders think like Margaret – that it could be an emergency but as nobody reacts, it probably is not. In this case, nobody acts in accordance with their private beliefs but in accordance to what they think is the belief of all others.

Even understanding that this is an emergency does not warrant that bystanders help. The presence of other people leads to *diffusion of responsibility*. The more bystanders there are around, the less each individual feels responsible to help. Studies have shown that the more people were around who could help in an emergency situation, the less likely it was that someone helped. When we come back to Kitty Genovese's death, neighbors did not refrain from helping *even though* there were so many people who could help but *because* there were so many people which led to diffusion of responsibility.

The Milgram study and the studies on helping behavior have been used to argue for the predictive power of situation in the person-situation debate.

THINKING ABOUT OTHERS: SOCIAL COGNITION

Some of the factors that lead to helping behavior include complex reasoning. For example, a bystander may assume that another person does not help because she thinks that this is not an emergency. Such reasoning includes cognitive processes reviewed in Chapter 2. Social psychologists built on the processes studied in cognitive psychology and established social cognition as a subfield.

Cognition includes perception, categorization, memory, judgment, and decision-making in general (see Figure 2.1). In social cognition, the same stages pertain to cognitive processes in relation to other people, that is, impression formation that includes perception and categorization, person memory, and social judgment.

When we meet an unknown person, it is important to form an accurate impression. People are often quite accurate in their impression of another person even if they see only minimal information. For example, 1-second silent video clips were sufficient to make judgments about sexual orientation of the filmed person with above chance accuracy (Ambady, Hallahan, & Conner, 1999). Judgments of likeability or trust from faces are done within 100 milliseconds. Indeed, judgments done from 100 ms exposures correlated highly with the same kind of judgments when the face was presented without time limit (Willis & Todorov, 2006).

The first impression of another person is often influenced by stereotypes, which include categorization of persons and groups. Categories are classes of objects that can be classified either on the basis of similarity (e.g., various kinds of birds) or on the basis of theories (e.g., all mammals breastfeed); in *stereotypes*, these objects are groups with which personal characteristics (e.g., criminal) or physical attributes (e.g., small) are associated. Stereotypes are categorizations and therefore purely cognitive representations. Yet when a stereotype pertains to a negative attribute, such as criminal, dumb, or lazy, it often is translated into *prejudice* which is the affective evaluation of members of a group.

We may think that it is easy to dismiss negative stereotypes because they are mere thoughts. However, it turns out that correcting stereotypes is not so easy. A classic study by Devine (1989) has shown that even participants who scored low on racism automatically used stereotypes that were processed unconsciously. Other studies, among them the popular Implicit Association Test (IAT; Greenwald, McGhee, & Schwartz, 1998), showed that people associate positive attributes with their own group (called ingroup) and negative attributes with another group (the outgroup). White people associate positive attributes with white people and negative attributes with black people; other studies show that black people associate positive attributes with black people and negative attributes with white people. Similar effects have been found when Japanese participants judge Koreans and Korean participants judge Japanese: in both groups, the ingroup is judged more positively than the outgroup. Like the study of Devine but with simpler means, the IAT shows that **stereotypes exist at an unconscious level.** Thus, stereotypes are difficult to correct and **people may unknowingly use them to form an impression** of another person.

When it comes to person memory, the **first impression is remembered best,** in line with the primacy effect discussed in the introduction. The first impression is also important because it determines the predictions – or hypotheses – about the future behavior of another person. From the subsequent behavior of the other person, individuals determine whether these hypotheses are true. As we have seen in Chapter 2, when people test hypotheses, they often commit a confirmation bias (Wason, 1960). This may lead to self-fulfilling prophecies, as the following experiment by Snyder, Tanke, and Berscheid (1977) revealed. They tested the assumption that attractive women may act friendlier because men think at the outset that they are friendlier than less attractive women. The researchers recruited male and female students. The men received a folder with information about the woman they were supposed to contact by phone, including a photograph. Half of the men got the picture of an extraordinarily attractive woman while the others got a picture of a less attractive woman. The photographs were not the actual depiction of the women with whom the men later talked on the phone. After viewing the picture, the men completed a questionnaire about character traits of the woman they were about to talk with. Indeed, men expected the allegedly attractive women to be more sociable, poised, humorous, and socially adept but unattractive women to be unsociable, awkward, serious, and socially inept. On the phone, men were also more sociable, warm, and independent when they believed they were talking to an attractive woman. As a consequence, the woman at the other end of the line became more sociable, poised, warm, and outgoing. By contrast, men thought that allegedly unattractive women were unsociable and serious and treated them in line with their expectations. These women, in turn, were indeed less friendly and sociable. This is a typical **self-fulfilling prophecy** where a person – here a man – first derives a hypothesis from available information and then acts accordingly. By this behavior, he elicits an interpretation and a response from the other person – here the woman – that confirms his hypothesis. The conversational cycle then starts again (see Darley & Fazio, 1980).

In their laboratory experiment, Snyder et al. made their students believe that the discussion partner is attractive or unattractive. However, the same may happen in the real world when attractiveness or lack thereof is part of the first impression when we meet another person. Such first impressions determine behavioral predictions that in turn guide our behavior because people commit the confirmation bias and therefore produce self-fulfilling prophecies.

Another instance of self-fulfilling prophecy is illustrated by a study conducted by Rosenhan (1973) where healthy people – among them a student, three psychologists, a painter, and a housewife – checked into psychiatric hospitals, alleging that they heard voices. In the hospital, they behaved normally and never again mentioned hearing voices. Aptly titled "Being sane in insane places," the study found that the alleged patients were released from hospital after 7 to 52 days; the average stay at the hospital lasted 19 days. It seemed that the staff, once they based their hypothesis on the first and only instance of hearing voices, interpreted the alleged patient's behavior in light of the assumption that he or she was mentally ill. This interpretation resulted in the maintenance of the belief that the alleged patient had a psychological disorder and had to stay in the hospital – a typical self-fulfilling prophecy. In some cases, patients in the hospital were quicker than the staff to find out that the alleged patient was not mentally ill.

Finally, humans judge other people. As reviewed in Chapter 2, people often use heuristics and fall prey to biases. One source of bias in social judgment is *illusory correlation*, which plays a role in the formation of stereotypes. In a classical study, students saw drawings allegedly made by patients with psychological disorders. Each drawing had a characteristic feature, such as big eyes, and was accompanied by a diagnosis, such as *paranoia*, which is the erroneous belief of being persecuted or the victim of a conspiracy. The materials were constructed such that features of the drawings did not correlate with any diagnosis. After students saw multiple pairings of drawings and disorders, they had to provide a judgment of how features of the drawings were related to specific diagnoses. Students thought that there were such relationships. For example, they thought that suspiciousness and hence paranoia is positively correlated to big eyes. As there was no real relationship, any perception of correlation is illusory (Chapman & Chapman, 1967). Interestingly, students without much knowledge of psychological disorders produced the same kind of relationships between characteristics and diagnoses as experts used in their clinical practice to assess the Draw-a-Person test. Nowadays, this test is largely discredited, as outlined in the next chapter. In the same way as in this classical study, people may generate illusory correlations between a group and an attribute, leading to exaggerated stereotypes.

Another process involved in judging people is causal attribution, which denotes the fact that when we see a person's action, we ascribe an underlying cause. For example, after a passenger shoved me in the bus, I may think that it happened when the bus stopped such that he shoved me accidentally. Alternatively, I may think that the passenger pushed me deliberately. Causal attributions are important because the interpretation of causes guides our action. This is not only true when causal attributions pertain to one's own performance, as we discussed in Chapter 3, but also when a person ascribes causes to behaviors of others. Especially when an action is negative and surprising, we almost automatically ask the question, "Why did he do it?"

The chapter so far seems to suggest that people obey when they should not, do not help when they should, automatically activate stereotypes that lead to prejudice, show judgmental biases, fall prey to self-fulfilling prophecies, and show judgmental biases. Although our perception, memory, and judgment may turn out to be wrong and sometimes lead to suboptimal action, we by and large get along well with other people. Remember Herbert Simon's (1990) notion of satisficing – that people do not maximize the quality of outcomes but are satisfied with a result that is good enough. Living in democratic countries, we are rarely confronted with demands as in the Milgram experiment. Although there are instances where we do not help when we should, these situations often include uncertainty. Studies show that people do help even in crowded trains when bystanders are certain that it is an emergency. Finally, many people are able to counter the effects of negative group stereotypes and judge other people as individuals.

HOW TO FIND AND KEEP A MATE

As should be known by now, psychologists explain behavior from multiple theoretical viewpoints. One viewpoint that has gained currency in the last three decades is evolutionary psychology. It starts from the assumption that inheritance explains a considerable part of the variance of behavior, as discussed in Chapter 4. Some behavior is better adapted to the environment. High adaptation increases the chances of survival and of finding a mate with whom an individual can produce offspring, which results in a higher probability of transmitting the genes that code this behavior to the next generation.

Evolutionary psychology deals with many aspects of human behavior, cognition, and emotion. The common underlying assumption is that the human mind consists of modules that serve a specific function, such as foraging, navigating through the environment, or finding a mate; these modules are domain specific. When it comes to finding a mate, the question arises whether mate preferences are the product of biological evolution or of socialization.

A good argument in favor of evolved preferences in human mate choice would be universality. If it could be shown that patterns of preference and choice are the same all over the world, it might strongly suggest that they are genetically transmitted across generations and therefore the product of evolution.

In a large-scale international study, David Buss (1989) examined mate preference and choice in 37 cultures. He started from asymmetries between the two sexes in having and raising offspring. As a first asymmetry, women are instrumental in raising children while men's contribution could be minimal – at the extreme, the act of procreation. Hence, while women can bear only one child per year, men could father many offspring. Moreover, women can be sure about their motherhood but men cannot be sure about their fatherhood. Finally, it is more difficult for women to raise children alone than together with a life companion who helps feed and protect the family. According to the tenets of evolutionary psychology, these asymmetries lead to an asymmetry of interests, namely men want to father as many children as they can but women want to secure the support of men for raising their children. From this asymmetry of interests, Buss predicted that women value good financial prospects more than men in women because in modern times, wealth helps secure the resources. This asymmetry of valuing financial prospects has a major consequence.

Men are more likely to be able to secure resources as they grow older; women are healthier and more fertile when they are young. Therefore, women desire older men to secure the necessary resources, and men desire younger women because of their good health and fertility. The desire for young, healthy women also means that men should be more interested in good looks, which serve as a sign of fertility and health. As men want to be sure that the offspring are their own, they are more likely to desire chastity in women than women in men. To summarize, from assumptions about universal consequences of sex differences, Buss predicted and found that across cultures, men prefer younger women with good looks and value chastity while women prefer older men who have good financial prospects. In all cases, the overwhelming majority of countries showed the predicted sex differences, and there were no significant differences in the other direction; for example, in no country did men prefer older women or women younger men. Factual age differences mirrored these preferences. In married couples, the husbands were on average older than their wives in each country where data were available.

Do these findings serve as evidence for an evolutionary stance? Although evolutionary psychologists see this study as a compelling confirmation of universality of biological sex differences and thus of the evolutionary nature of preferences, adherents of social role theory – introduced in the previous chapter – claimed that it is still possible to explain the data with cultural gender roles. They pointed to the fact that the sex differences found in Buss's study differed across cultures. These differences seemed to be related across variables – that is, in cultures where there were greater sex differences in preferred age of the spouse, there were also greater sex differences in desired financial prospects, good looks, and chastity. When it came to the latter variable, many countries did not show significant differences. More importantly, there were not only sex differences but also differences among cultures, and the cultural differences were more pronounced than the sex differences. In Spain, for example, the mean preference on a scale from 0 (unimportant) to 3 (important) for a chaste partner was 0.66 for men and 0.36 for women. By comparison, in Iran, the same preference was 2.67 for men and 2.23 for women. Although there was a significant sex difference in both countries, the cultural difference between Spain and Iran is much larger. In Spain and other Western countries, chastity is unimportant for both men and women. By contrast, it is important for both sexes in Iran and other non-Western countries. The observation that cultural differences sometimes exceed sex differences favors an interpretation in terms of gender roles.

Another means to doubt a biological basis of sex differences is to show that these differences depend on cultural factors. In a re-analysis, Eagly and Wood (1999) correlated Buss's data with two measures of gender equality. They found that greater gender equality correlated negatively with gender differences; the more equal a society, the smaller were the gender differences in financial prospects, good looks, and preferred age.

Although the universality in the observed differences between men and women is uncontroversial, the nature of these differences is debated. Evolutionary psychologists advocate a biological approach that assumes genetic transmission of preferences and natural selection for particular genetic dispositions that are adapted to the environment. They think of these differences as *sex differences* based on human biology. Socio-cultural explanations start with the assumption that societies define social roles for men and women; then, behaving according to gender roles results in gender differences. They claim that the observed differences are *gender differences* based on human culture.

The studies on human mate preferences tell us how two individuals select each other and what makes them attractive at the outset. Yet what keeps two individuals together after they have found each other? What keeps a partner attractive? In other words, what is the nature of love?

When Linda, an undergraduate college student, enthusiastically tells her roommate that she fell in love with a fellow student, her feeling most often covers one aspect of love that is called *passion* and is based on romantic feelings and physical attraction. However, passion is not sufficient to maintain love because it often wanes over time. Psychologists have identified other components that are necessary to preserve a loving relationship. Sternberg (1986), for example, distinguished three components of love: passion, commitment, and intimacy. While passion is short-lived, the other two components can explain love in the long term. Research shows that the most powerful predictor of relationship satisfaction in long-term relationships is *commitment*. It seems that the conscious decision to commit oneself to this and only this relationship helps overcome the relative lack of passion that comes in after some time.

Intimacy is the gradual development of mutual understanding and a feeling of closeness. Couples do not seem to notice intimacy in a long-term relationship until they miss it. This fact may explain the observation that some divorced couples miss each other when they are separated for some time. Such longing is difficult to account for by commitment that the couple has given up.

Although there are different conceptualizations of the term love (see Berscheid, 2010; Reber, 2016), all classifications distinguish between at least two main components. The first component includes passion and sexual attraction and is relatively short-lived. The second component includes mutual understanding – part of Sternberg's intimacy component – and commitment and is relatively long-lived. In summary, passion may be a kind of catalyst that helps to initiate the loving relationship and to maintain it for the first couple of months. During this time, mutual understanding and commitment have to develop to bring forth a long-lasting relationship.

LIVING IN GROUPS

The theories reviewed so far have one characteristic in common: they do not analyze social relationships. When we looked at studies that demonstrated the power of the situation, social cognition or theories of human attraction, psychologists investigated processes in the individual mind. Even the theory of self-fulfilling prophecy considers cognitive processes in two individual minds. An exception is the previous section, where love is investigated from the viewpoint of mutual passion, commitment, and intimacy in two individuals.

Instead of analyzing cognitive and affective processes in individuals, researchers may analyze social processes in groups. This section first reviews an influential theory of social relations and then considers two important group processes: cooperation as examined by social dilemmas and intergroup conflict.

A *group* consists of two or more individuals who are connected to each other by relatively enduring social relationships (see Forsyth, 2014). Within a group, behaviors emerge that cannot be observed in individuals. For example, groups may share resources, develop hierarchies, or develop procedures for voting and contributions to the common good. According to Fiske's (1992) theory of social relations, there are four basic models of human social relations: communal sharing, authority ranking, equality matching, and market pricing. Let us illustrate the four forms of social relations with the example of eating a meal together with others.

Communal sharing is best exemplified when we think of a potluck, where each brings food according to their ability and each eats according to their needs. *Authority ranking* means that there is a clear hierarchy within a group, with the highest-ranking members making the decisions. When eating a meal, the highest-ranked group member can choose first and determine who gets what and how much. *Equality matching* can be seen in situations where food is scarce. The group determines that each member gets the same amount of food. For example, when there are three sausages for six family members, each one gets half of a sausage. Finally, *market pricing* can be illustrated by a restaurant visit where each guest gets food in accordance to what they have paid for.

In the last few decades, scientists have studied dilemmas linked to social relations and cooperation within communities. Well-known is the "tragedy of the commons" (Hardin, 1968). Some traditional villages had shared pastures (the commons) where every farmer could let his cattle graze. This is an example of cooperation based on communal sharing: every farmer could use the commons according to his needs. This goes fine as long as every farmer has a limited number of cows or sheep, but it becomes a problem if too many cattle overgraze the commons. At that point, a dilemma emerges. For the individual farmer, it is most rational to have as much cattle as possible and to send them all to the commons in order to get the most out of the shared land. For the community, by contrast, the freedom to graze cattle on the commons results in overuse and, in the end, the destruction of the pasture. As individuals in such a situation act according to what is most rational for them in the short term, regulations are needed to secure what is most rational for the community in the long term.

A well-known example in modern society is overfishing in the ocean. For the individual fisherman, it is most rational to catch as much fish as possible, but it leads to depletion of the fishing grounds.

Regulations are necessary to stop overuse and allow fishing grounds to recover. One could think of various solutions along Fiske's social relations model. For example, giving the privilege of catching fish to some but not to others would amount to authority ranking. More popular measures in the Western Hemisphere are either equality matching (each fisher can catch a limited but equal amount of fish) or market pricing (fishermen have to buy a license to catch a limited amount of fish; limiting the number of licenses limits the number of licensed fishermen and therefore overuse of the fishing grounds).

In order to examine economic dilemmas, scientists have developed economic games to observe decision-making in individuals. Games involving hierarchy and therefore authority ranking are the ultimatum game and the dictator game. In the *ultimatum game*, one player (the proposer) is told that she can share an amount of money, say $10, with another player (the responder). She is free to divide the amount as she wishes, but the responder can decide whether he wants to accept the offer. If he does, both players get the amount as divided by the proposer. If the responder rejects the offer, none of the players gets any money. The most rational thing to do for the proposer is to keep as much money as possible, say, $9. The most rational decision for the responder would be to accept even a minimal amount, here $1, because he would be one dollar richer, which is better than nothing. However, this is not what experimenters observe. On average, the proposer offers somewhat less than half of the money. The most frequent offer is 50 percent, but the average is often between 30 and 40 percent. Moreover, the responder only accepts offers that are not too remote from fair division of the amount (for an overview of findings, see Camerer, 2003). It seems that many players adhere to norms of equality matching when playing the ultimatum game.

It seems obvious that the proposer in the ultimatum game has to offer a minimal amount because the receiver can reject it and also does so when the offer is too far from equal sharing. However, what happens if a proposer can divide the money without any possibility for the recipient to reject the offer? This is the *dictator game*. In this game, keeping all money would be the most rational option for the proposer. Yet this is not what most participants do. Even in this game, only around 20 to 30 percent of the proposers keep all money for themselves. However, if the proposers were assured that the experimenter would not know how they allocated the money, more than 60 percent of the proposers kept all the money.

Although some players adhere to the norm of equality in cooperative games, others do not; they try to be free riders. Letting people get away with free riding may have the detrimental effect that it is no longer rational to cooperate and other people start defecting from cooperation. How can a community or society secure that all people adhere to norms of fair contribution to the community?

The answer is *altruistic punishment*, which means that people are willing to punish others for free riding even if punishment is costly. In a study by Fehr and Gächter (2002), participants in a group of four could contribute money to a common pot. The game was set up such that it was in the interest of the individual to keep the money but in the interest of the group as a whole to share it. If all contributed, everybody earned more. If some individuals contributed but others did not, those who contributed lost and those who did not contribute gained. If a person did not cooperate, other participants could decide to punish the defector, but at a cost; they had to sacrifice additional money to punish. Indeed, participants often punished those who did not cooperate. In another session, the group played the same game but without the opportunity to punish. The authors observed that when participants could punish, group members cooperated but cooperation broke down when there was no opportunity to punish in the face of defection. There is a problem, however, reminiscent to diffusion of responsibility in helping behavior. When others are around who could punish a defector, why should I incur the cost? If everybody eschews responsibility and waits for the others to punish, nobody will punish defectors in the end. Remember the case of the subway employee who rebuked a young man for smoking. He paid a heavy price for telling the young man about the smoking ban, but his deed qualifies as altruistic punishment that helps society to maintain its laws and norms and to maintain cooperation within a group.

Cooperation does not only increase group benefits but may help resolve conflicts between groups, or *intergroup conflict*. One hypothesis states that two groups that know each other are less prejudiced and prone to conflict than groups that do not know each other. In order to prevent or to solve intergroup conflict, it may be beneficial to bring the two groups together; this is the *contact hypothesis*. In the classical "Robbers Cave" study, the contact hypothesis was tested in a summer camp for boys at a remote place in Oklahoma, Robbers Cave State Park (Sherif, Harvey, White, Hood, & Sherif, 1961). Twenty-four boys were assigned to two groups. In the first stage of the experiment, team spirit within each group was cultivated by giving them tasks that required cooperation. After having achieved cohesion within each group, experimenters created competition between the two groups. In this second stage, the boys participated in various group contests, which soon led to a high degree of conflict between the two groups.

In the third stage, the experimenters changed the arrangement so that the boys no longer competed but had to cooperate to achieve superordinate goals. For instance, the experimenters interrupted the water supply to the camp, and the boys of both groups had to work together to repair it. The results of the change from competition to cooperation were striking. Conflicts stopped and the relationship among the boys across the two groups improved. Note that the study also showed that to stop hostilities, it was not enough to organize joint activities the boys enjoyed, such as watching movies; cooperation was a necessary ingredient to stop conflict. The main conclusion from this and other research on the contact hypothesis is that contact between two different groups increases conflict when the groups compete against each other but decreases conflict when they cooperate with each other.

Let us apply this main finding to the school context. In an analysis of the classroom situation, Elliot Aronson (2002) concluded that it is characterized by competition. Each student sits in class and is concerned about his own grades, especially when a curve of the class grade makes visible where he stands in comparison to his fellow students. When the teacher asks a question, 6 to 10 out of 20 students compete for attention by raising their hand; all but the one student called on by the teacher will be disappointed.

Social comparison and competition result in an unpleasant classroom that lacks compassion and team spirit. The situation became explosive when schools in Austin, Texas, started desegregated schooling such that black and Hispanic children were bused to schools in white middle-class areas. As the minority children came from lower-class neighborhoods with substandard schools, they performed worse than the white middle-class children. When the white children outperformed the minority children and let them know it, fistfights broke out and the classroom atmosphere was at its lowest; it looked like minority children were the losers of desegregation.

To respond to this situation, Aronson developed in the early 1970s a method called *jigsaw classroom*. Instead of working individually, students work together on a task that is relevant for a later exam. However, group work is not enough, as it may lead to social loafing. In addition, if the most motivated or most gifted children in a group bear the brunt of the work, they will resent those who work less. It is therefore crucial that the task is arranged in a way that every group member has to contribute her share, and every student needs to listen to everybody else in the group because the knowledge each group member contributes is relevant for a subsequent exam. Thus, when the most gifted children tease an academically disadvantaged group member, it is often sufficient to remind the children that the information provided by the disadvantaged child is relevant to the exam. The necessity to collaborate for the exam leads children to develop techniques to ask good questions and to help each other. In a field experiment, students who spent 8 weeks in the jigsaw classrooms showed more confidence, liked school better, were less absent, and performed better compared to children who received standard instruction. A more precise analysis showed that the minority students improved most while the white students performed equally well as before the intervention. These studies reveal the potential to alleviate intergroup conflict when individuals from diverse backgrounds cooperate with each other.

Recommended literature

Overview

Aronson, E., Wilson, T.D., & Akert, R.M. (2015). *Social psychology* (9th ed.). Boston, MA: Pearson/Allyn and Bacon.

Classical primary sources

Darley & Latané (1968; see references).
Greenwald et al. (1998; see references).
Milgram (1963; see references).

8

PSYCHOLOGICAL DISORDERS AND THEIR TREATMENT

Research in psychology explores the causes of behavior in people. In our example of the young smoker at the subway station, there may be several possible reasons for his aggression. We discussed, among others, lack of punishment, observation of aggressive models, brain damage, immaturity, and lack of self-control. However, which of these possible causes is the real one that made the individual at the subway station attack the employee who told him not to smoke? Clinical psychologists have to deal with the causes of individual behavior. They have to answer two questions: Why did a person do what he did? And second, how could a therapy change undesired behavior? In addition, clinical psychologists have to adhere to ethical principles. For example, it would be unethical to impose psychotherapeutic treatment on a patient if the patient objects to it.

In the first section, we discuss what the term *abnormal* means and what methods clinicians use to diagnose psychological disorders. The next section presents an overview on psychological disorders and discusses some difficulties in classifying them. We then turn to psychotherapy and discuss general principles of evidence-based interventions and specific approaches to treat psychological disorders.

WHAT IS ABNORMAL?

Beyond the young smoker's aggression, there are other examples of behavior we may consider abnormal. A young woman, Elaine, has become reclusive, rarely leaves her home, and quit her job even though she needs the money to make a living. She avoids any place where she could meet other people and does not answer voice messages. She tells an aunt that she is anxious all day. Then you meet William – a successful writer of fiction – at three receptions and observe him drinking too much. You wonder if he is an alcoholic. In all three cases, you think that something is abnormal. Yet what does "abnormal" mean? And how do clinicians assess abnormality?

Criteria for abnormality

There are three main criteria to label a behavior abnormal. It means that a person experiences suffering from his condition (distress), that his behavior harms himself or others (dysfunction), or that the behavior does not accord to statistical or social standards (deviance).

Distress is an obvious criterion. We have seen in Chapter 3 that most people are happy most of the time. By contrast, long-enduring or intense suffering is a sign that something has gone wrong and might be a sign of abnormality. Most people with mental disorder experience distress, for example delusions, anxiety, panic attacks, or trauma. Clinicians have to distinguish distress that indicates a psychological disorder from distress that is normal, such as intense grief after the death of a parent, spouse, or child. In this case, grief is not seen as abnormal unless it worsens over time, leading to feelings of emptiness, avoidance of social relationships, and ultimately to depression.

Distress is a useful criterion in many but not all cases of abnormality. Individuals with pedophilia and so-called antisocial personality disorders, in everyday language labeled psychopaths, usually do not suffer as a consequence of their behavior. However, society deems their behavior abnormal because it causes harm in others – it is dysfunctional.

Dysfunction is the second criterion for abnormality and means that a person's behavior harms themselves or others. Dysfunctional behavior interferes with everyday routines, such as caring for oneself, having normal social contacts, or being able to work. For example, being afraid of a dangerous dog is a healthy reaction, and nothing needs to be done about the person. Being afraid of dogs in general becomes a problem when the dogs are not dangerous and a person takes measures that hamper her daily life, such as taking long detours or even staying at home to avoid dogs in the neighborhood.

In the extreme, dysfunction can mean danger for the person herself or others. Some patients die as a consequence of anorexia, an eating disorder, or from suicide caused by depression. However, a condition does not need to be classified as a psychological disorder in order to be dysfunctional. Studies show that loneliness is more mortal than smoking, excessive drinking, obesity, pollution, or lack of exercise (Holt-Lunstad, Smith, & Layton, 2010). While mortality can be a direct consequence of anorexia and depression, the mortality due to loneliness is more indirect. As the evidence is only correlational, it is unclear what mechanism causes the mortality of loneliness. For example, loneliness may lead to depression in some patients, and depression results in higher mortality. Alternatively, a third variable may increase both loneliness and mortality. One could imagine that a person who suffers from physical disability has both a higher likelihood of being lonely and higher mortality. In this last case, loneliness does not cause mortality but is only correlated to mortality because of a common cause, here physical disability. Despite being dysfunctional, loneliness itself is not a disorder but can be best understood as a cause or consequence of a disorder that increases mortality.

In contrast to depictions in popular culture, individuals with psychological disorders, even if they include delusions or bizarre thinking, are rarely an immediate danger to themselves or others.

Deviance – the third criterion of abnormality – means that a person's behavior is not within the limits defined by standards. There are two main kinds of standards: statistical and social norms. Statistical standards most easily can be illustrated by standardized intelligence tests. An IQ lower than 70 on the Stanford-Binet test is considered impaired or delayed (mildly impaired or delayed between IQ 60 and 69), whereas people with an IQ higher than 130 are considered gifted or very advanced (see Kaufman, 2009). Remember that IQ tests are standardized such that the population mean is 100 and one standard deviation is 15. An IQ of 70 is two standards deviations below the mean, which means that 2 to 3 percent of the population is classified as intellectually impaired. Note that by this definition relative to the population, we will never be able to eradicate intellectual impairment because there will always be 2 to 3 percent of the population at the lowest end, regardless of the absolute level of intellectual ability. Likewise, an IQ of 130 is two standard deviations above the mean, which means that 2 to 3 percent of the population is classified as intellectually gifted. While impairment is seen as a problem, giftedness is not. Intellectual impairment is considered abnormal by society because it may lead to dysfunction, such as low school performance and lack of employability. By contrast, giftedness is beneficial for the individual and society.

Deviance from statistical norms does not always contradict social norms; giftedness is neither dysfunctional nor considered deviant by society. On the other hand, deviant behavior as defined by social norms may not be rare. Until the mid-20th century, American society defined premarital sex as deviant – the social norm said not to do it. At that time, Alfred Kinsey started surveys on sexual practices in the United States. To the surprise of many, he found out that premarital sex was quite common among young Americans. He showed that deviance in terms of social norms was not necessarily deviant in statistical terms. Clinicians have to take care not to classify a behavior as a disorder only because it is against social norms.

In the early 20th century, clinicians like German psychiatrist Emil Kraepelin began to describe abnormal behaviors and classify them as mental disorders. Modern classifications of mental disorders include the International Classification of Diseases (ICD) by the World Health Organization and the Diagnostic and Statistical Manual of Mental Disorders (DSM) by the American Psychiatric Association. The most recent versions are the ICD-10 (ICD-11 is in preparation at the time of writing) and DSM-5. These classification systems have undergone change. For example, homosexuality by itself neither leads to distress nor to dysfunction in daily life. Nevertheless, homosexuality was classified as a psychological disorder until the 1970s when the American Psychiatric Association replaced it with sexual orientation disorder for people in conflict with their sexual orientation. Nowadays, homosexuality is no longer seen as a deviance from social norms, and therefore it is no longer listed as a psychological disorder in the DSM. Such changes show how much the notion of deviance and hence the classification of disorders depends on cultural values.

How can we link what we know about abnormality to the examples discussed at the beginning of the section? The young smoker at the subway station may not suffer, but attacking others for being told that smoking is prohibited certainly is dysfunctional behavior: it harms others and deviates from social norms. Elaine *seems* to meet – we have to be careful with our assumptions – two criteria for abnormality: distress and dysfunction. She is anxious all day, which makes her distressed and suffering. As she has quit her job and can no longer support herself financially, her reclusiveness is also dysfunctional. When it comes to William's drinking, it seems to contradict social norms – it is deviant. Excessive drinking may lead to dysfunction in the long run. We shall come back to William's drinking later.

Diagnosis of psychological disorders

How do psychiatrists or psychologists assess whether a person suffers from a psychological disorder? The most prominent assessment methods are clinical interviews, clinical tests, and clinical observation (see Comer, 2013).

Usually, people come to a psychotherapist and tell her the reason they seek treatment. The psychotherapist first conducts a clinical interview. In this face-to-face conversation, she collects information about the client's personal details and background, such as profession, marital status and family, problems, stressors, thoughts and feelings. Interviews provide the therapist with personal information, but they may lack validity. People often do not want to touch embarrassing topics, and they may provide biased information. It is well-known, for example, that depressive people often view themselves in a more negative light than others do.

Clinical tests include two broad types of assessments: self-report scales and projective tests. Self-report scales measure symptoms and characteristic thoughts, feelings, and behaviors of patients. There are general scales, like the *Minnesota Multiphasic Personality Inventory* (MMPI), which measures various clinically relevant dimensions, and scales for specific disorders. An example of a specific scale is the *Beck Depression Inventory*. It instructs clients to choose from response alternatives such as "I don't have any thoughts of killing myself," "I have thought of killing myself but I would not carry it out," "I would like to kill myself," and "I would kill myself if I had the chance." These tests adhere to the same strict reliability and validity criteria as the personality and intelligence tests reviewed in the previous chapter.

Projective tests aim to make diagnoses through a more indirect route. Projective tests got their name from the belief of clinicians that when clients interpret or draw a picture, they project their problems into the interpretation or production of the materials. Clinicians hoped to unravel hidden problems through their clients' responses.

Let us look at two famous examples. The first is the *Rorschach test* – constructed by Swiss psychiatrist Hermann Rorschach – which consists of 10 symmetric inkblots. The test-taker is presented with the inkblots, one by one, and is instructed to tell what the inkblots look like. The psychologist interprets the answers according to more than hundred characteristics under the assumption that the person projects unconscious conflicts and problems into the inkblots.

A second projective test is the *Draw-a-Person test*. The test-taker is instructed to draw a person, and the psychologist tries to extract a diagnosis from characteristics of the drawing, assuming that problems of the client are projected into the drawing. There are two main scoring systems: one that looks at the drawing as a whole and the other that looks at isolated features of the drawing, such as large eyes as an indication of psychopathology. In the previous chapter we saw that students without expertise in clinical psychology construct illusory correlations between features and relevant pathological states, such as big eyes and paranoia. In fact, experts seem to do the same. Although still used in practice, projective tests have the problem that they have low validity and are therefore poor indicators of psychological disorders. Some of them seem to be based on illusory correlations. Most importantly, they do not possess *incremental validity*, which means that they do not add useful information above and beyond tests that are easier to administer and score (see Lilienfeld, Wood, & Garb, 2000).

Finally, *clinical observation* may include naturalistic observation, analog observation, and self-monitoring. *Naturalistic observation* takes place in the environments where clients usually live or work, such as home or school but also hospitals or prisons. Often, a so-called participant-observer – a key person who lives or works with the client – records behavior and reports to the clinician. For example, the mother of an aggressive child may record every instance of disruptive or aggressive behavior.

When naturalistic observation is not possible, people may be placed in a special environment, such as a laboratory or research kindergarten equipped with one-way mirrors or video cameras where clinicians observe and record behavior. This is *analog observation*. Clinical observation may lack inter-rater reliability – two observers may focus on different aspects of behavior and therefore arrive at different conclusions. A threat to validity is *observer bias*, which denotes the fact that observations are guided by information or expectations, in line with the confirmation bias and self-fulfilling prophecies. These threats to reliability and validity make it obvious that observers need to be well trained to prepare them for their task.

Self-monitoring means observation of one's own behavior. When a person has a drinking problem, he may monitor when he drinks, how much, and at which occasions. A behavior therapist, who tries to change behavior according to the principles of operant conditioning (Chapter 1), can then see what triggers drinking and plan the therapeutic intervention accordingly.

In the first part of this section, we learned the criteria for abnormality: distress, dysfunction, and deviance. The second part of the section briefly outlined how clinicians try to diagnose disorders from clinical interviews, tests, and observation. These assessments are now and again plagued with threats to reliability and validity. Why is it not possible to diagnose psychological disorders with more precision?

PSYCHOLOGICAL DISORDERS

When a patient visits the general practitioner with chest pain and shortness of breath, the doctor can take x-rays and conduct a blood test to find out whether the patient suffers from pneumonia, lung cancer, or another ailment. Psychiatrists and psychologists, on the other hand, have to make a diagnosis from the symptoms without recourse to biological data that reveal the causes of the disease (see McNally, 2011). Moreover, as discussed in Chapter 4, neurological diseases but not psychological disorders are distinguishable from each other through their genetic makeup (Anttila et al., 2018).

Behaviorists assume that conditioning is at the root of some conditions, such as anxiety; cognitive psychologists postulate mental processes that lead up to a disorder; neuroscientists look into brain processes and behavioral geneticists at processes of genetic transmission to find out what the cause is. However, the causes of psychological disorders have remained obscure. This makes it hard to diagnose psychological disorders or to confirm a diagnosis. The Rosenhan study mentioned in the previous chapter illustrates this point. If the doctors in the mental hospital had had diagnostic tests at their disposal, they easily could have found out that the alleged patients simulated the disease.

Another problem is *comorbidity*, which means that a disease occurs together with another disease. Comorbidity in psychological disorders, for example depression and anxiety, is usually high. In medicine, pneumonia and lung cancer are distinct diseases, even if they occur together. However, the lack of diagnostic tests that unequivocally discriminate between two psychological disorders makes it difficult to determine whether these are two disorders or just one.

Some researchers have even questioned whether disorders made up of bundles of symptoms exist at all. Instead of looking for a disorder behind a cluster of symptoms, we might analyze the relationships among symptoms and identify risky clusters that need therapeutic intervention without thinking of a psychological disorder as a neatly identifiable disease. This approach to psychopathology is called *network analysis* (Borsboom & Cramer, 2013).

Despite such problems, clinicians began to classify psychological disorders, as we saw in the previous section. Both ICD-10 and DSM-5 classify psychological disorders purely based on symptoms, without recourse to causal explanations. Clinicians try to find the causes of the disorder for each individual by collecting information on problems, stressors, or early childhood experiences through interviews, clinical tests, or observation.

It follows an overview of some prominent psychological disorders (for more detailed information, see Comer, 2013): autism, schizophrenia, depressive disorders, bipolar disorder, anxiety disorders, obsessive-compulsive disorders, posttraumatic stress disorder (PTSD), eating disorders, substance-related and addictive disorders, and attention deficit/hyperactivity disorder (ADHD).

Autism spectrum disorder is a psychological condition that appears early in life, often before the age of 3. Most of the afflicted – 80 percent of them boys – suffer as adults from severe disabilities and have enormous difficulties working and living independently. Children with autism spectrum disorder show marked impairment in social interaction; they are extremely unresponsive and do not communicate. Some evidence points to deficiencies in perspective taking and empathy. Moreover, autistic children execute rigid and repetitive routines or rituals that seem meaningless to the outside world.

The history of this disorder illustrates the damage that could be done by unfounded speculations on the causes of mental disorders. The psychiatrist who described autism first, Leo Kanner (1943), offered the psychoanalytical explanation that it is caused by "refrigerator parents," especially cold mothers. You can imagine how much guilt such an assumption caused in mothers of autistic children. Empirical research has never supported this assumption but found instead biological factors related to autism, such as a reduction of activity in so-called mirror neurons in the brain that are related to perspective taking and empathy (Oberman et al., 2005). As it is a multifaceted disorder, mirror neurons certainly are not the only cause of autism spectrum disorder, and research on biological causes is just at its beginning.

Autism does not necessarily lead to dysfunction. Some children suffering from one form of autism, called Asperger's disorder, develop some of the social deficits characteristic of autism but function at a normal or near-normal level. They may become successful at jobs that require attention to detail and limited social interaction.

Schizophrenia is a disorder characterized by cognitive and emotional deficits and delusions. People with schizophrenia often have visual or auditory *hallucinations*; that is, they see images and hear voices that do not exist. Hallucinations may have different content, most frequently of being persecuted and plotted against, but also delusions of grandeur, such as being Jesus, or the belief of patients that their own feelings, thoughts, and actions are controlled by others. Other symptoms of schizophrenia include disorganized speech, restricted emotional expression, social withdrawal, and *catatonia*, a condition characterized by restricted movement or bizarre poses. Although little is known about the causes of schizophrenia, genetic and brain research suggests a strong biological component.

Although schizophrenia is a debilitating condition, sufferers may be highly intelligent, as the example of mathematician John Nash shows. He began academic work in his twenties, then fell ill, and resumed his work after spending several years in psychiatric clinics. He won the Nobel Prize in Economics and is immortalized in the book and movie *A Beautiful Mind*.

Most people who suffer from a *depressive disorder* (or *depression*) feel sad, dejected, and empty. Some people suffer from *anhedonia*, which is the inability to experience pleasure. They lack drive and initiative, are usually less active, spend more time alone, blame themselves for misfortunes, even when they are not responsible for the outcome, and consider themselves inadequate and inferior. Depression can be a fatal disorder because it is the most important predictor of suicide.

Depression is a quite common disorder. A large-scale epidemiological study in the United States with almost 10,000 respondents showed that *lifetime prevalence* – that is, the percentage of adults who suffer from clinically relevant depression at least once during their lifetime – is around 17 percent (for this and the following details on lifetime prevalence, see Kessler et al., 2005). There are various hypotheses on the causes of depression, among them genetic disposition and learned helplessness.

Bipolar disorder includes mood swings between depression and *mania*; the latter is an elevated mood state that includes inflated self-esteem, decreased need for sleep, talkativeness, racing thoughts, distractibility, and increased activity.

There is a wide range of *anxiety disorders*. Some people are worried often and in most situations. These people suffer from *general anxiety disorder*. Some people, by contrast, fear a specific object; they suffer from *specific phobia*. There are dozens of such phobias, but among the most prominent ones are fear of enclosed spaces like elevators (*claustrophobia*), heights (*acrophobia*), and spiders (*arachnophobia*), which is one of innumerable phobias related to animals, such as *ophiophobia* (fear of snakes) and *kynophobia* (fear of dogs). People who suffer from *social phobia* have severe, persistent, and unfounded fears of social situations that may lead to embarrassment, such as speaking in public. People with anxiety disorders normally know that their fears are excessive and unreasonable.

The lifetime prevalence for anxiety disorder is more than 20 percent. The *1-year prevalence* of a disorder tells us what percentage of the population is affected within a given year. For generalized anxiety disorder, large-scale epidemiological studies in the United States found that this number is 4 percent, which means that in a given year, 4 out of 100 inhabitants suffer from this disorder. Only about 25 percent of those people receive clinical treatment. The 1-year prevalence for specific phobia is almost 9 percent, and for social phobia it is around 7 percent. Only about 20 to 25 percent of the afflicted receive clinical treatment.

Obsessive-compulsive disorders consist either of *obsessions*, which are unwanted thoughts or images that intrude a person's consciousness, such as the impulse to yell obscenities in public or to imagine forbidden sexual acts; or *compulsions*, which are repetitive acts or thoughts that people think they have to perform in order to prevent or reduce anxiety. For example, people afraid of contamination may wash their hands or vacuum their house excessively, often for hours each day. These individuals understand that their compulsion is meaningless. Despite their rational insight, however, they are unable to leave behind their compulsive habit. Lifetime prevalence for obsessive-compulsive disorder is between 1 and 2 percent.

Posttraumatic stress disorder (PTSD) denotes a disorder people develop that is triggered by severe trauma, such as being a victim of rape or being involved in a serious accident or in gory combat. Symptoms are recurrent intrusive memories, dreams, flashbacks, a sense of reliving the experience, and distress or physical arousal when reminded of the traumatic event. Further repercussions of PTSD are sleeping difficulties, irritability, poor concentration, hypervigilance, and an exaggerated startle response. About 7 percent of adult Americans have experienced PTSD once in their lifetime.

The most frequent *eating disorders* are *anorexia* and *bulimia nervosa*. At the core of both disorders is a morbid fear of being overweight. As normal-weight women are more dissatisfied with their body than men, and thinness has become an ideal, it is no wonder that the prevalence of eating disorders increased since the 1960s. Anorexia occurs most often in girls and young women aged 14 to 18. They refuse to keep their body weight above the minimal normal weight. Research points to distorted perception of their body size and a narrow focus on weight and body shape in self-evaluation.

People with bulimia have recurrent episodes of binge eating followed by inappropriate compensatory behavior, such as self-induced vomiting, to prevent weight gain; like individuals with anorexia, they too are overly concerned with body shape and weight. Although occasional binge eating has been observed in about half of students in the United States, and self-induced vomiting in about 15 percent (see Lakin & McClelland, 1987), only a fraction of these qualify for the diagnosis of bulimia nervosa that requires at least one episode of binge eating and inappropriate compensatory behavior per week for 3 consecutive months. There is much overlap in the characteristics of individuals with anorexia and bulimia but also some differences. Most importantly, due to their different practices to prevent weight gain, anorexic people usually are underweight, whereas bulimic people keep their weight at or above the minimal normal weight.

Substance-related and addictive disorders are related to the use of both legal drugs, such as alcohol, and illegal drugs. The lifetime prevalence of these disorders is almost 15 percent, with alcohol use disorder being the most prevalent at more than 13 percent. People with a substance-related or addictive disorder experience symptoms such as developing tolerance for the drug, which means that drug consumers need higher doses of the drug to attain the same effects; consumption of the drug even if it leads to severe interference with everyday life, such as drinking even if it impairs family life or performance at study or work; strong cravings for the drug; and withdrawal symptoms when a person stops taking the drug.

Finally, *attention deficit/hyperactivity disorder* (ADHD) denotes a condition where children have difficulty paying attention and are often distracted (attention deficit) and disturb their environment with frequent fidgeting, running and wandering around, interrupting others, and excessive talking (hyperactivity).

These are just the most prominent disorders. Other psychological disorders include disorders of childhood and adolescence; personality disorders, including paranoid personality disorder characterized by paranoia; stress disorders; somatic symptom disorders where physical symptoms have psychological causes; sexual disorders; and gender identity disorder.

An increasing problem in psychiatry and clinical psychology has been overdiagnosis. In terms of signal detection theory (Table 2.1), there are too many false alarms because clinicians judge a disorder to be present when in fact it is not. In recent decades, more and more conditions have been included in the DSM classification. This has led to a situation where more and more people fall within the boundaries of a psychiatric diagnosis, which led some critics to fear that millions of people with normal conditions, such as grief after bereavement, reacting to stress, eating too much, having tantrums in childhood, or forgetting in old age, will be diagnosed with psychological disorders (see Wakefield, 2016).

A case in point is ADHD. One in five high school boys and 11 percent of all US schoolchildren are diagnosed with ADHD. Two-thirds of them receive medication for the disorder. There is evidence that these figures are caused by overdiagnosis. For example, the youngest children in a class are diagnosed more often with ADHD. As there is no indication that ADHD is unevenly distributed across birth dates, it seems that the least developed children within a class get diagnosed with ADHD (see Wakefield, 2016). Moreover, ADHD rates increase dramatically when schools get incentives to increase test scores, for two reasons. First, these children are entitled to receive special classes and services, which may raise their test scores. Second, in some school districts, test scores of children who have ADHD do not count; this provides an incentive to diagnose academically poor children with ADHD in order to increase a school's average test scores (Hinshaw & Scheffler, 2014).

Let us come back to some of the examples introduced at the beginning of the previous section. Couldn't we now classify each of them – the young smoker, Elaine, and William – according to their respective disorders? This is problematic for various reasons. What disorder does the young smoker have? We don't know. Aggression as a symptom does not point to a specific disorder, and many people who are aggressive from time to time do not have a disorder as defined in the DSM or ICD systems. This does not mean that there is no problem, but not every problem is related to a psychological disorder. What about the reclusive Elaine? Does she suffer from social phobia or depression? From the description we have, we cannot know because identical symptoms may fit different disorders. Although we have some indications that Elaine suffers and her condition hampers her daily life, we have to check whether her symptoms are severe enough to qualify for a disorder at all. William seems to have a clear case of substance abuse, more specifically, alcohol use disorder. Yet be careful. First, you have seen him three times at receptions where people drink – and he drank too much. However, he may have normal drinking habits in everyday life. Strong indicators of alcohol use disorder may be regular drinking at work or drinking in the morning after getting up. A second reason to be careful is comorbidity. For example, alcohol abuse may be caused by underlying depression. Therapists might then have to tackle depression as the primary problem, not alcoholism. The example of William is based on a real person – William Styron, the author of the award-winning novel *Sophie's Choice*. He also wrote a small book that many consider as one of the best literary accounts of depression (Styron, 1990; see also *The Bell Jar* by Sylvia Plath, 1971).

GENERAL PRINCIPLES OF PSYCHOTHERAPY

When people suffer from psychological disorders or experience problems, they are referred to psychotherapy. The clients meet a trained therapist who uses psychological principles to treat their specific disorder or problems (see Wampold & Imel, 2015). Psychotherapy offered by psychologists differs from two other kinds of treatment: from general interventions not aimed at specific treatment but at improving general well-being, such as meditation or relaxation; and from medical treatments offered by medically trained psychiatrists.

From a medical perspective, psychological disorders have biological causes. Psychiatrists therefore prescribe drugs to improve the condition. Medication revolutionized psychiatry in the 1950s when so-called neuroleptics were developed. These drugs did not cure schizophrenia, but they reduced the symptoms to a point that patients could be released from psychiatric units and only returned when they had an acute episode. Often patients receive a combination of drugs and psychotherapy, and both have been proven effective. In contrast to medical treatments, psychotherapy relies exclusively on psychological mechanisms, such as learning and thinking about problems and understanding them.

Both medical and psychological approaches to the treatment of psychological disorders are evidence-based. In order to test the effectiveness of psychotherapy, researchers use experimental designs with randomized assignment of participants to treatment and control groups, as explained in Box 8.1.

Box 8.1 Testing the effectiveness of psychotherapy

When psychotherapists want to explore whether a psychotherapeutic intervention is effective, they compare patients who receive therapy to patients in a control group who do not. Patients in the control group are often on a waiting list for treatment. In *randomized controlled trials* (RCT), there are two or more treatment conditions to which participants are randomly assigned and for which the outcomes, such as improvement of symptoms, are measured and compared.

When a new therapy is tested, it is not only of interest whether the new technique works in comparison to patients who have no treatment but also in comparison to the best treatment available to date. If the new treatment is superior, it may replace the old one; if it has the same effect, therapists have an additional treatment option; if it is less effective, the traditional treatment remains in place.

One of the biggest problems in psychotherapy research is the effect of *allegiance*, which is the degree to which a psychotherapist believes in the effectiveness of a treatment. Allegiance biases therapy outcomes in the direction of the psychotherapists' beliefs and preferences. It is therefore important to control for allegiance. In fact, after allegiance is taken into account, differences between treatments often disappear.

There is ample evidence from randomized controlled trials that psychotherapy works. However, we saw in the previous section that a medical approach to diagnose psychological disorders is not feasible because there are no clearly identifiable causes that could distinguish between two kinds of disorders. Why, then, does psychotherapy work?

To answer this question, the distinction between common factors and specific factors has been introduced. *Common factors* are those variables that make every psychotherapy work, regardless of their specific assumptions and methods. An important common factor is *alliance*, the working relationship between client and the psychotherapist. Alliance includes mutual trust and agreement on goals and tasks within the therapy. For example, ratings of therapist empathy consistently predict how positive the therapy outcome will be. A second common factor is the *expectation of the client* that the therapy will be effective. Therapists often explain to their clients what they do and how their treatment will help alleviate the negative symptoms. Part of the positive effect of expectation can be explained by *remoraliza-*

tion, which denotes the observation that clients show an improvement of their condition after they made an appointment with the psychotherapist but before they begin therapy.

Effects of common factors are reminiscent to the placebo effect that we discussed in Chapter 4. The effects of placebo are unspecific and related to the fact that a patient expects the treatment to have positive effects. Finally, even interventions thought to be targeted at a specific disorder may have beneficial general effects. For example, different therapies may postulate different underlying mechanisms, but all therapies may have in common that they change dysfunctional thought and therefore lead to healthy outcomes. In this case, changing dysfunctional thoughts would be a factor common to all therapies across disorders, not a specific factor.

We have mainly considered client effects – alliance, expectation, and remoralization. However, research shows that some therapists are better than others; the difference between effective and less effective therapists is large in the long run. This observation raised the question about what the therapist effects might be. Wampold and Imel (2015) list interpersonal skills such as warmth and empathy. As we have seen, therapist empathy contributes to alliance. Another therapist skill that predicts early alliance is self-doubt – a kind of humbleness and sensitivity that helps a therapist reflect on her own practice and revise the course of therapy if necessary (Nissen-Lie, Monsen, & Rønnestad, 2010).

Specific factors include those ingredients within a therapy that are targeted at the specific symptoms or underlying mechanisms of the disorder, such as depression or phobia. As we have seen earlier, the problem is that we know little about the underlying mechanisms of the specific psychological disorders, and comorbidity is high. In contrast to the common factors, it has been difficult to find specific factors that make psychotherapy more effective. In medical treatment, you would expect that the specific treatment causes the healing effect while it does not make much of a difference which doctor provided the treatment. However, in psychotherapy the effect of the therapist is much larger than the effect of the specific treatment. To conclude, common factors are much more important than specific factors for therapy outcomes.

The observation that common factors explain most of the effects of psychological treatment means that there is no big difference in effectiveness between specific psychotherapy methods. Alluding to *Alice in Wonderland*, where the Dodo bird said after a race, "Everybody has won and all must have prizes," Rosenzweig (1936) noted that all kinds of psychotherapies have similar outcomes. This conjecture has been dubbed the *Dodo bird effect*, and evidence so far seems to support it.

Let us end this section with a methodological point. When researchers examine the effectiveness of a therapeutic method, one study is not enough. Studies differ in method, characteristics of the sample, severity of symptoms, cultural background, and other variables. It is therefore imperative to see whether an effect is valid across studies. It is often difficult to know whether the overall outcome is positive because some studies show positive outcomes, others no differences between treatment and control group, still others positive outcomes for one group but not for others, and finally, one or the other study may even find negative outcomes. In order to get a measure of overall effectiveness, researchers conduct meta-analyses (see Box 8.2).

Box 8.2 Is an effect stable across studies? Meta-analysis

Psychologists have adopted meta-analysis, a statistical technique that allows an overall conclusion based on all available comparisons between clients who received treatment and clients who did not. To conduct a meta-analysis, a researcher has to collect all available studies that performed the comparison of interest. The first researchers to use meta-analysis in clinical psychology were interested in whether psychotherapy is effective compared to no therapy (Smith & Glass, 1977). They collected all studies available at that time – 375 studies with 833 individual effects in total – that compared psychotherapy with a control group without therapy. From the size of the effect derived from each comparison between therapy group and control group, Smith and Glass computed the mean effect size across all studies and assessed whether the difference was significantly different from zero. The authors found that psychotherapy leads to better outcomes than no therapy. This meta-analysis refuted earlier claims that psychotherapy is not effective.

Beyond comparing various forms of psychotherapy to a non-treatment control group, the question arises whether some form of therapy, for example behavior therapy, is better than others, such as psychodynamic approaches. However, refuting earlier claims by psychotherapists, Smith and Glass found that the different forms of therapy had similar effects and all showed better outcomes than no therapy – confirming the Dodo bird effect discussed earlier.

Later meta-analyses confirmed that the overall effect for comparisons between psychotherapy and no therapy control was considerable; the treated person will have a better outcome than 76 percent of the untreated patients (for a summary, see Wampold & Imel, 2015).

To summarize, meta-analyses allow researchers to calculate the size of an effect across multiple studies and to conclude whether the difference between two conditions is significant.

In conclusion, psychotherapy is better than no therapy, but all therapies seem to have comparable effects – that is, there is not one form of therapy that is superior to others, and even for specific diagnoses there seem to be few differences in the effectiveness of therapeutic approaches. In fact, it turns out that the therapist contributes more to the effect than the therapy method.

APPROACHES TO PSYCHOTHERAPY

Different approaches in psychology developed various forms of psychotherapy that influence its practice to this day. These approaches differ in what they consider as problem, as improvement, and the method best suited to achieve the improvement. We review the four main therapeutic approaches: behavior, cognitive, psychodynamic, and humanistic.

Behavior therapy

Behavior therapy was derived from behaviorism and follows the learning principles reviewed in Chapter 1. They see dysfunctional behavior as the problem and consider it an improvement if such behavior disappears. For example, Liza's excessive fear of dogs is dysfunctional and therefore problematic. The improvement consists in the extinction of the fear.

Behavior therapists developed various methods to achieve extinction of maladaptive behavior. Two well-known techniques to treat anxiety are systematic desensitization and exposure therapy (see Wolpe, 1973). *Systematic desensitization* starts from the assumption that when a fear-arousing stimulus comes to mind, it leads to anxiety which is a negative state. Relaxation, by contrast, is a positive state and therefore incompatible with anxiety. If a person thinks of a fear-arousing stimulus while in a relaxed state, the stimulus should lead to a more positive response. The client first has to learn a relaxation technique. Then the therapist asks the client to write down a list of his fears. He then ranks the fears in accordance to their severity. The therapy begins with the least intense fear. The client has to relax and then to imagine the fear-arousing object. When the client loses his fear of the least feared object, he proceeds to the next object and so on until the fear of the most intense stimulus is eliminated or at least alleviated. One may object that it is just the regular practice of relaxation that makes people less fearful, not its connection to the fearful stimulus. However, this is not the case. Relaxation needs to be paired with the fear-arousing stimulus in order to replace the negative response with a positive one.

A second method to alleviate anxiety is *exposure therapy*. The rationale is simple: when Liza avoids contact with dogs for fear of being bitten, contact with dogs that do not bite extinguishes the fear response. Especially popular among therapists is *flooding*, a specific technique of exposure therapy where patients are in contact with the feared object most of the time for an extended period. Liza would be around dogs for some days; a man with social phobia goes with his therapist to all kinds of populated places, such as restaurants, concerts, and parties, for some days; and a woman with claustrophobia rides elevators or squashes into narrow spaces, again for a few days and several hours per day. Flooding is an effective method to extinguish fear.

Cognitive therapy

People not only behave; they also think. Right at the beginning of the cognitive revolution (see Chapter 2), clinicians like Aaron Beck and Albert Ellis began to investigate distorted thought in patients with psychological disorders and developed *cognitive therapy*. Cognitive therapists start from the assumption that a situation triggers thoughts that influence behavior. More technically, thoughts mediate the effect of the situation on behavior. Moreover, thoughts in the form of appraisals of the situation influence emotions that in turn influence behavior. Therefore, irrational thinking may lead to excessive, inappropriate emotions and dysfunctional behavior. For example, Liza's excessive fear of dogs is irrational because she overestimates the danger of dogs. Therefore, irrational thought is the problem and therapists aim their efforts at correcting distorted thought to improve the client's problem.

A cognitive therapist first has to find out a patient's cognitive distortions. Beck (1963) interviewed depressive clients and compared their thoughts with non-depressed individuals. He found not only differences in the contents of the thoughts, such as low self-regard, self-blame and suicidal wishes in depressive patients, but also systematic biases of thinking. Instances are *overgeneralization* (for example a man who thinks that minor mishaps at work prove his inadequacy for the job) and *minimization* and *maximization* (for example the inclination of a high school girl to think that the many teachers who are friendly to her are insincere but that the few teachers who are unfriendly are sincere; the significance of friendliness is minimized and the significance of unfriendliness maximized).

After the patient's distortions are known, the therapist tries to correct them. Beyond creating a therapeutic relationship that results in alliance and positive expectations, the therapist addresses the cognitive distortions by showing the patient that perceived reality is not necessarily reality itself, and that interpretation of reality can be faulty. Patients learn how their own thoughts are self-defeating. It is common that the therapist disputes the irrational beliefs of the patient and tries to change them. By changing the beliefs, patients begin to interpret situations differently, which results in changes of their emotions, in line with appraisal theories of emotion discussed in Chapter 3.

Nowadays, many therapists use *cognitive-behavioral therapy*, which is a combination of cognitive and behavior therapy. For example, Liza's therapist may use exposure therapy combined with challenging irrational thoughts connected to her fear of dogs. Such a combination seems natural because the two forms of therapy complement each other. Behavior therapy aims to change behavior while cognitive therapy aims to change thoughts.

Psychodynamic therapy

Psychodynamic therapy (often used interchangeably with *psychoanalysis*) started with the works by Sigmund Freud and is the historically earliest psychotherapeutic approach. Therapists in this tradition consider the problem to be the result of unconscious desires or fears that are expressed in phantasies in childhood and lead to unconscious conflicts in adulthood. These desires and fears remain unconscious because they touch forbidden topics, for example sexual desires. Therefore, the person tries to exclude these wishes from consciousness, a process called *repression*. As the client has no access to the unconscious conflicts, psychodynamic therapy aims to uncover and understand these repressed thoughts. Insight into the previously hidden conflicts is supposed to improve the client's problem.

Two main methods are used to uncover unconscious conflicts: *free association*, where the patient tries to report his uncensored thoughts; and *dream interpretation*. Psychoanalysts assume that unconscious conflicts remain hidden in waking thought but are expressed in dream contents. However, patients are often reluctant to acknowledge the desires that surface during analysis – a process called *resistance*. Moreover, patients often redirect feelings resulting from unconscious childhood conflicts toward the therapist. This process is called *transference*. For example, a woman who has been sexually abused as a child and as a result avoids close contacts with other people might fear that the therapist abuses her trust in him. Patients have to overcome resistance and transference in order to arrive at a full understanding of the underlying conflicts. This understanding is then supposed to reduce maladaptive thought and behavior.

Psychoanalysis has been criticized because many of its concepts like dream interpretation or repression – and others not discussed here but well-known in popular culture, such as Oedipus complex, castration anxiety, and penis envy – received little empirical support. Despite the lack of empirical support for some of its traditional core concepts, psychodynamic therapy is as effective in improving maladaptive thought and behavior as other forms of therapies. It does not seem that the specific ingredients that make psychodynamic therapies unique contribute to the therapy outcome but that psychoanalysts are as good at building a trusting therapeutic relationship as therapists trained in other forms of therapy.

If we look more closely at psychodynamic approaches, we notice that the principle of getting insights into one's problems could be understood in terms of cognitive processes. Indeed, Aaron Beck, one of the founders of cognitive therapy, was trained as a psychoanalyst, and modern psychodynamic approaches refer to cognitive theories to explain the process of therapeutic understanding. There remain nevertheless important differences between the two approaches. Most importantly, psychodynamic theories assume that unconscious conflicts expressed in one's early childhood phantasies influence one's thoughts and feelings as an adult, whereas cognitive therapists assume that patients have a learning history leading to erroneous patterns of thought and dysfunctional emotions. Second, psychoanalysts assume that conflicts are unconscious and patients do not have access to sources of dysfunctional feelings and behavior. Cognitive therapists, by contrast, take it for granted that clients have access to their thoughts and inner conflicts and can reflect on them. Finally, the two therapeutic approaches differ in their methods. Psychodynamic therapists let the patient explain, and the therapist sometimes provides interpretations, whereas cognitive therapists actively try to change the thoughts of their patients.

Humanistic approaches to therapy

What behavioral, cognitive, and psychodynamic therapies have in common is the assumption that psychotherapy addresses an underlying dysfunction that has to be cured. This notion is derived from the medical model. By contrast, *humanistic approaches* to psychotherapy do not consider psychotherapy as repair of a broken mechanism but as helping clients to fulfill their potential. The therapist does not provide a diagnosis, and it is the client himself who has to find the means to cultivate personal growth or to end a crisis. Remember Maslow's (1943) stage of self-actualization. A person values new experiences, nurtures creativity, and entertains high moral standards. Such a person is autonomous, thinks independently, and strives for personal growth and meaning. Therapists in the humanist tradition are convinced that their clients aim for self-actualization, and that they possess all resources within themselves to realize this aspiration.

In order to enable the client to find out about his resources, the therapist listens. Carl Rogers (1951) developed *client-centered therapy*, which has three core conditions. First, the therapist has to be *genuine* and does not hide behind a professional façade. She must be interested in a real understanding of the client. Second, the therapist has *unconditional positive regard* for the client. She accepts the client as he is and does not evaluate his thoughts and feelings. The third core condition is *empathic understanding* of the client's concerns, which means that the therapist tries to understand the client from his own viewpoint and senses meaning that the client is scarcely aware of.

An important consequence of the three core conditions is the non-directive nature of the dialog between therapist and client. While behavioral and cognitive therapists give direct instructions and psychoanalysts provide interpretations of what clients tell them, client-centered therapists listen and usually do not even direct the client to one or the other topic. A therapist only asks questions to make sure that she properly understood the client. Therapists in the humanist tradition are confident that their non-directive approach to therapy, embedded in genuineness, unconditional regard, and empathic understanding, enables the client to find his own means to cultivate personal growth and find meaning.

Outlook

You may have asked why there are different schools of psychotherapy after research has found that the therapist contributes more to the therapy outcome than the therapy method. As discussed in the previous section, common factors such as alliance, expectations, and remoralization are much more important than specific factors. However, most therapy methods emerged before meta-analysis was introduced to therapy research, so that the therapeutic schools were established before psychotherapy research started. Nowadays, many therapists have begun to use integrative approaches; that is, they combine effective elements from different schools to optimize therapy outcomes (see Castonguay, Eubanks, Goldfried, Muran, & Lutz, 2015). Hence, the main focus of therapy research is no longer which school of therapy offers the best treatment but which methods are the most effective to help clients reach their goals – either to reduce suffering from dysfunctional thought and behavior or to increase personal meaning and inner growth.

Recommended literature

Overviews (from which much of this chapter was drawn)

Comer (2013; see references).
McNally (2011; see references).
Wampold & Imel (2015; see references).

Classical primary sources

Rosenhan (1973; see references).
Smith & Glass (1977; see references).

EPILOGUE

Why we do what we do

We have now reviewed the basics of psychology. We have seen that behavior can be explained from the viewpoint of different theoretical approaches. Such explanations include learning from experience, thinking about the consequences, motivation, genetic transmission, early childhood events, personality, or the situation. The question is not "who is right" but how much does each component contribute and how do they interact. When we addressed the nature-nurture debate, we saw that genes influence the choice of the environment and culture influences the extent of universal sex differences in mate preferences. Regarding the person-situation debate, there is evidence for the power of both personality and situational factors in predicting behavior.

Psychologists combine elements of the various approaches to explain mind and behavior. An example of such an integrative concept is *attitude*, which is defined as the mental representation of an evaluation of an object that is stable over time and has cognitive, affective, and behavioral components. We may have stable attitudes about such different attitude objects as Amazon, liberals, eating meat, or gaming.

There are some overarching theories that try to explain behavior as affected by multiple causes. An example is the theory of planned behavior (Ajzen, 1991).

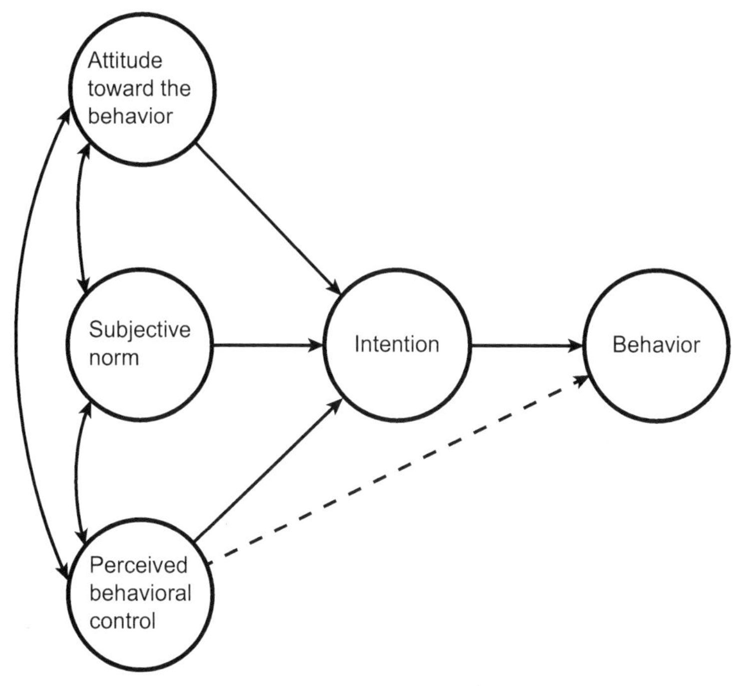

Figure 9.1 Theory of planned behavior
Source: From Ajzen, I. (1991).

The theory of planned behavior has been widely tested and is useful to predict, for example, health and environmental behavior. Although Paul wants to stop his addiction, he may still like smoking but feels social pressure from his girlfriend, among others. Yet he knows that he cannot control the urge. This lack of control prevents the desired change even though it would be in line with his and others' attitudes. Sarah, on the other hand, may think it is pleasant to fly to remote vacation destinations (attitude), and she may not feel social pressure because her neighbors do the same (subjective norm). She does not restrict flying even if she were fully able to do so (behavioral control). In this example, the lack of personal attitude and social pressure prevents behavior that would help the environment. Although there is much data on the influence of single variables on thought and behavior, comprehensive models that include several predictors will become more common. Moreover, the increase in computational power in the past few decades has made it possible to perform complex statistical analyses, supporting the development and assessment of ever more complex models.

Despite the trend to more complex models that presumably have higher ecological validity, psychology as a science has been criticized, both from inside and outside its mainstream.

Criticism by an insider comes from Rozin (2006). He notes that current mainstream psychology as an academic field examines processes, for example perception, memory, thought, or emotion. This focus on mental processes leads to the neglect of what is really interesting in everyday life, such as eating, sex, entertainment, politics, and religion. These phenomena are difficult to address by examining simple processes. To turn to these issues, Rozin proposes to conduct more descriptive research, like biologists do. When it is known what people do in real life researchers can begin to study the underlying processes in the laboratory.

Another criticism from scholars from the humanities is reminiscent to the one Hermann Ebbinghaus encountered over 130 years ago. Human thought, feeling, and behavior are too complicated for scientific research. Psychologists may find some isolated effects and correlations, but they can never understand humans as a whole. Scientific psychology looks at the human mind from a third-person perspective – an objective outside perspective – in the same way that medicine looks at the body or a mechanic looks at a car engine. What we miss is the first-person perspective to find out what gives inner meaning to human existence. We can explain behavior, but we do not understand the person in a deeper sense.

It is true that psychology has objectified the human mind in the same way medicine has objectified the human body. On the one hand, this approach has proven successful. Thanks to medicine, life expectancy more than doubled in the last 200 years, and few people wish to return to a time without vaccines, antibiotics, and pharmacological pain relief. Scientific psychology, too, improved the lives of people. To mention just a few examples, people with mental health problems no longer are told that they lack willpower; there is a trend to use more motivating and effective teaching methods at school;

job applicants are less exposed to invalid assessment methods such as unstructured interviews; and psychological research has contributed to improve cooperation and conflict resolution.

On the other hand, despite success and progress, psychologists must humbly admit that they do not consider the person as a whole; there may be layers of meaning in human existence that science cannot dissect.

REFERENCES

Ainsworth, M.D.S., & Bell, S.M. (1970). Attachment, exploration, and separation: Illustrated by the behavior of one-year-olds in a strange situation. *Child Development*, *41*, 49–67.

Ainsworth, M.D.S., & Bowlby, J. (1991). An ethological approach to personality development. *American Psychologist*, *46*, 333–341.

Ajzen, I. (1991). The theory of planned behavior. *Organizational Behavior and Human Decision Processes*, *50*, 179–211.

Allport, G.W. (1958). What units shall we employ? In G. Lindzey (Ed.), *Assessment of human motives* (pp. 239–260). New York, NY: Holt, Rinehart, & Winston.

Allport, G.W., & Odbert, H.S. (1936). Trait-names: A psycho-lexical study. *Psychological Monographs*, *47*(1), whole issue.

Ambady, N., Hallahan, M., & Conner, B. (1999). Accuracy of judgments of sexual orientation from thin slices of behavior. *Journal of Personality and Social Psychology*, *77*, 538–547.

Anderson, C.A., Lindsay, J.J., & Bushman, B.J. (1999). Research in the psychological laboratory: Truth or triviality? *Current Directions in Psychological Science*, *8*, 3–9.

Annas, J. (2011). *Intelligent virtue*. Oxford: Oxford University Press.

Anttila, V., Bulik-Sullivan, B., Finucane, H.K., Walters, R.K., Bras, J., Duncan, L., . . . Patsopoulos, N.A. (2018). Analysis of shared heritability in common disorders of the brain. *Science, 360*(6395), eaap8757.

Aronson, E. (2002). Building empathy, compassion, and achievement in the jigsaw classroom. In J. Aronson (Ed.), *Improving academic achievement: Impact of psychological factors on education* (pp. 209–225). San Diego, CA: Academic Press.

Baillargeon, R. (1987). Object permanence in 3½-and 4½-month-old infants. *Developmental Psychology, 23*, 655–664.

Bakermans-Kranenburg, M.J., Van IJzendoorn, M.H., & Juffer, F. (2003). Less is more: Meta-analyses of sensitivity and attachment interventions in early childhood. *Psychological Bulletin, 129*, 195–215.

Bandura, A. (1965). Influence of models' reinforcement contingencies on the acquisition of imitative responses. *Journal of Personality and Social Psychology, 1*, 589–595.

Bandura, A. (1977). Self-efficacy: Toward a unifying theory of behavioral change. *Psychological Review, 84*, 191–215.

Barker, R., Dembo, T., & Lewin, K. (1941). *Studies in topological and vector psychology: Vol. II: Frustration and regression: An experiment with young children*. Iowa City: University of Iowa Press.

Bartlett, F.C. (1932). *Remembering: A study in experimental social psychology*. Cambridge: Cambridge University Press.

Beck, A.T. (1963). Thinking and depression: I: Idiosyncratic content and cognitive distortions. *Archives of General Psychiatry, 9*, 324–333.

Berkowitz, L. (1989). Frustration-aggression hypothesis: Examination and reformulation. *Psychological Bulletin, 106*, 59–73.

Bernstein, I.L., & Webster, M.M. (1980). Learned taste aversions in humans. *Physiology & Behavior, 25*, 363–366.

Berscheid, E. (2010). Love in the fourth dimension. *Annual Review of Psychology, 61*, 1–25.

Birbaumer, N., Ghanayim, N., Hinterberger, T., Iversen, I., Kotchoubey, B., Kübler, A., . . . Flor, H. (1999). A spelling device for the paralysed. *Nature, 398*(6725), 297.

Borsboom, D., & Cramer, A.O. (2013). Network analysis: An integrative approach to the structure of psychopathology. *Annual Review of Clinical Psychology, 9*, 91–121.

Breiman, L., Friedman, J.H., Olshen, R.A., & Stone, C.J. (1984). *Classification and regression trees*. London: Routledge.

Buss, D.M. (1989). Sex differences in human mate preferences: Evolutionary hypotheses tested in 37 cultures. *Behavioral and Brain Sciences, 12*, 1–49.

Camerer, C.F. (2003). *Behavioral game theory: Experiments in strategic interaction*. Princeton, NJ: Princeton University Press.

Cannon, W. (1927). The James-Lange theory of emotions: A critical examination and an alternative theory. *American Journal of Psychology, 39*, 106–124.

Carlson, S. (1985). A double-blind test of astrology. *Nature, 318*(6045), 419–425.

Carpenter, P.A., Just, M.A., & Shell, P. (1990). What one intelligence test measures: A theoretical account of the processing in the Raven Progressive Matrices Test. *Psychological Review, 97*, 404–431.

Castonguay, L.G., Eubanks, C.F., Goldfried, M.R., Muran, J.C., & Lutz, W. (2015). Research on psychotherapy integration: Building on the past, looking to the future. *Psychotherapy Research, 25*, 365–382.

Chalmers, D.J. (1996). *The conscious mind: In search of a fundamental theory*. Oxford: Oxford University Press.

Chapman, L.J., & Chapman, J.L. (1967). Genesis of popular but erroneous psychodiagnostic observations. *Journal of Abnormal Psychology, 72*, 193–204.

Comer, R.J. (2013). *Abnormal psychology* (8th ed.). New York, NY: Worth.

Costa, P.T., Terracciano, A., & McCrae, R.R. (2001). Gender differences in personality traits across cultures: Robust and surprising findings. *Journal of Personality and Social Psychology, 81*, 322–331.

Darley, J.M., & Fazio, R.H. (1980). Expectancy confirmation processes arising in the social interaction sequence. *American Psychologist, 35*, 867–881.

Darley, J.M., & Latané, B. (1968). Bystander intervention in emergencies: Diffusion of responsibility. *Journal of Personality and Social Psychology, 8*, 377–383.

DeCasper, A.J., & Fifer, W.P. (1980). Of human bonding: Newborns prefer their mothers' voices. *Science, 208*(4448), 1174–1176.

Deci, E.L. (1971). Effects of externally mediated rewards on intrinsic motivation. *Journal of Personality and Social Psychology, 18*, 105–115.

Deci, E.L., Koestner, R., & Ryan, R.M. (1999). A meta-analytic review of experiments examining the effects of extrinsic rewards on intrinsic motivation. *Psychological Bulletin, 125*, 627–668.

Deci, E.L., & Ryan, R.M. (1985). *Intrinsic motivation and self-determination in human behavior*. New York, NY: Plenum Press.

Devine, P.G. (1989). Stereotypes and prejudice: Their automatic and controlled components. *Journal of Personality and Social Psychology, 56*, 5–18.

Diener, E., & Diener, C. (1996). Most people are happy. *Psychological Science*, 7, 181–185.

Dollard, J., Miller, N.E., Doob, L.W., Mowrer, O.H., & Sears, R.R. (1939). *Frustration and aggression*. New Haven, CT: Yale University Press.

Duckworth, A.L., Peterson, C., Matthews, M.D., & Kelly, D.R. (2007). Grit: Perseverance and passion for long-term goals. *Journal of Personality and Social Psychology, 92*, 1087–1101.

Dutton, D.G., & Aron, A.P. (1974). Some evidence for heightened sexual attraction under conditions of high anxiety. *Journal of Personality and Social Psychology, 30*, 510–517.

Eagly, A.H., & Wood, W. (1999). The origins of sex differences in human behavior: Evolved dispositions versus social roles. *American Psychologist, 54*, 408–423.

Ebbinghaus, H. (1913/1885). *Memory: A contribution to experimental psychology* (H. Ruger & C. Bussenius, Trans.). New York, NY: Teachers College Press.

Eccles, J.S., & Wigfield, A. (2002). Motivational beliefs, values, and goals. *Annual Review of Psychology, 53*, 109–132.

Eisenberg, N. (2000). Emotion, regulation, and moral development. *Annual Review of Psychology, 51*, 665–697.

Ekman, P., & Friesen, W.V. (1971). Constants across cultures in the face and emotion. *Journal of Personality and Social Psychology, 17*, 124.

Erikson, E.H. (1994/1959). *Identity and the life cycle*. New York, NY: W. W. Norton.

Fawl, C.L. (1963). Disturbances experienced by children in their natural habitats. In R.G. Barker (Ed.), *Century psychology series: The stream of behavior: Explorations of its structure & content* (pp. 99–126). East Norwalk, CT: Appleton-Century-Crofts.

Fehr, E., & Gächter, S. (2002). Altruistic punishment in humans. *Nature*, *415*(6868), 137–140.

Ferster, C.B., & Skinner, B.F. (1957). *Schedules of reinforcement*. East Norwalk, CT: Appleton-Century-Crofts.

Firestone, C., & Scholl, B.J. (2016). Cognition does not affect perception: Evaluating the evidence for "top-down" effects. *Behavioral and Brain Sciences*, *e229*.

Fiske, A.P. (1992). The four elementary forms of sociality: Framework for a unified theory of social relations. *Psychological Review*, *99*, 689–723.

Flynn, J.R. (1987). Massive IQ gains in 14 nations: What IQ tests really measure. *Psychological Bulletin*, *101*, 171–191.

Fodor, J.A. (1983). *The modularity of mind*. Cambridge, MA: MIT Press.

Forsyth, D.R. (2014). *Group dynamics* (6th ed.). Belmont, CA: Wadsworth Cengage Learning.

Fredrickson, B.L. (2001). The role of positive emotions in positive psychology: The broaden-and-build theory of positive emotions. *American Psychologist*, *56*, 218–226.

Friedman, H.S., & Kern, M.L. (2014). Personality, well-being, and health. *Annual Review of Psychology*, *65*, 719–742.

Funder, D.C. (2013). *The personality puzzle*. New York, NY: W. W. Norton.

Garcia, J., & Koelling, R.A. (1966). Relation of cue to consequence in avoidance learning. *Psychonomic Science*, *4*, 123–124.

Gottfredson, L.S. (2004). Intelligence: Is it the epidemiologists' elusive "fundamental cause" of social class inequalities in health? *Journal of Personality and Social Psychology*, *86*, 174–199.

Greenwald, A.G., McGhee, D.E., & Schwartz, J.L.K. (1998). Measuring individual differences in implicit cognition: The implicit association test. *Journal of Personality and Social Psychology*, *74*, 1464–1480.

Greifeneder, R., Bless, H., & Fiedler, K. (2018). *Social cognition: How individuals construct social reality* (2nd ed.). Hove: Psychology Press.

Hardin, G. (1968). The tragedy of the commons. *Science*, *162*(3859), 1243–1248.

Harlow, H.F. (1958). The nature of love. *American Psychologist*, *13*, 673–685.

Hauser, R.M., & Palloni, A. (2011). Adolescent IQ and survival in the Wisconsin longitudinal study. *Journals of Gerontology Series B: Psychological Sciences and Social Sciences*, *66*(S1), I91-I101.

Havighurst, R.J. (1974). *Developmental tasks and education* (3rd ed.). New York, NY: David McKay.

Hertwig, R., & Ortmann, A. (2001). Experimental practices in economics: A methodological challenge for psychologists? *Behavioral and Brain Sciences*, *24*, 383–403.

Hinshaw, S.P., & Scheffler, R.M. (2014). *The ADHD explosion*. New York, NY: Oxford University Press.

Holt, N., Bremner, A., Sutherland, E., Vliek, M., Passer, M., & Smith, R. (2015). *Psychology: The science of mind and behavior* (3rd ed.). London: McGraw-Hill.

Holt-Lunstad, J., Smith, T.B., & Layton, J.B. (2010). Social relationships and mortality risk: A meta-analytic review. *PLoS Medicine*, *7*, e1000316.

Hugdahl, K., & Öhman, A. (1977). Effects of instruction on acquisition and extinction of electrodermal responses to fear-relevant stimuli. *Journal of Experimental Psychology: Human Learning and Memory*, *3*, 608–618.

Hull, C.L. (1943). *Principles of behavior: An introduction to behavior theory*. Oxford: Appleton-Century.

Iyengar, S.S., & Lepper, M.R. (1999). Rethinking the value of choice: A cultural perspective on intrinsic motivation. *Journal of Personality and Social Psychology*, *76*, 349–366.

James, W. (1884). What is an emotion? *Mind*, *9*, 188–205.

John, O.P., & Srivastava, S. (1999). The Big-Five trait taxonomy: History, measurement, and theoretical perspectives. In L.A. Pervin & O.P. John (Eds.), *Handbook of personality: Theory and research* (Vol. 2, pp. 102–138). New York, NY: Guilford Press.

Johnson, E.J., & Goldstein, D. (2003). Do defaults save lives? *Science*, *302*(5649), 1338–1339.

Jung, C.G. (2016/1921). *Psychological types*. London: Routledge.

Kahneman, D. (2011). *Thinking fast and slow*. New York, NY: Farrar, Straus and Giroux.

Kahneman, D., & Deaton, A. (2010). High income improves evaluation of life but not emotional well-being. *Proceedings of the National Academy of Sciences*, *107*, 16489–16493.

Kanner, L. (1943). Autistic disturbances of affective contact. *Nervous Child*, *2*, 217–250.

Kanwisher, N., McDermott, J., & Chun, M.M. (1997). The fusiform face area: A module in human extrastriate cortex specialized for face perception. *Journal of Neuroscience*, *17*, 4302–4311.

Kaufman, A.S. (2009). *IQ testing 101*. New York, NY: Springer.

Kessler, R.C., Berglund, P., Demler, O., Jin, R., Merikangas, K.R., & Walters, E.E. (2005). Lifetime prevalence and age-of-onset distributions of DSM-IV disorders in the National Comorbidity Survey Replication. *Archives of General Psychiatry*, *62*, 593–602.

Kim, K.H., Relkin, N.R., Lee, K.M., & Hirsch, J. (1997). Distinct cortical areas associated with native and second languages. *Nature*, *388*(6638), 171–174.

Kuhn, T.S. (1962). *The structure of scientific revolutions*. Chicago, IL: University of Chicago Press.

Kuncel, N.R., & Hezlett, S.A. (2010). Fact and fiction in cognitive ability testing for admissions and hiring decisions. *Current Directions in Psychological Science*, *19*, 339–345.

Kuncel, N.R., Hezlett, S.A., & Ones, D.S. (2004). Academic performance, career potential, creativity, and job performance: Can one construct predict them all? *Journal of Personality and Social Psychology*, *86*, 148–161.

Lakin, J., & McClelland, E. (1987). Binge eating and bulimic behaviors in a school-age population. *Journal of Community Health Nursing*, *4*, 153–164.

Langer, E.J. (1975). The illusion of control. *Journal of Personality and Social Psychology*, *32*, 311–328.

Lashley, K.S. (1950). In search of the engram. In *Society for experimental biology: Physiological mechanisms in animal behavior: (Society's Symposium IV.)* (pp. 454–482). Oxford: Academic Press.

LeDoux, J. (1996). *The emotional brain*. New York, NY: Simon and Schuster.

Lenneberg, E.H. (1967). *The biological foundations of language*. Oxford: Wiley.

Libet, B. (1985). Unconscious cerebral initiative and the role of conscious will in voluntary action. *Behavioral and Brain Sciences*, *8*, 529–539.

Lilienfeld, S.O., Wood, J.M., & Garb, H.N. (2000). The scientific status of projective techniques. *Psychological Science in the Public Interest*, *1*, 27–66.

Loftus, E.F. (1979). *Eyewitness testimony*. Cambridge, MA: Harvard University Press.

Lorenz, K.Z. (1937). The companion in the bird's world. *The Auk*, *54*, 245–273.

Maier, S.F., & Seligman, M.E. (1976). Learned helplessness: Theory and evidence. *Journal of Experimental Psychology: General*, *105*, 3–46.

Marañon, G. (1924). Contribution à l'étude de l'action émotive de l'adrenaline. *Revue Française de l'Endocrinologie*, *2*, 301–325.

Maslow, A.H. (1943). A theory of human motivation. *Psychological Review*, *50*, 370–396.

Maurer, D., & Werker, J.F. (2014). Perceptual narrowing during infancy: A comparison of language and faces. *Developmental Psychobiology*, *56*, 154–178.

Mazur, J.E. (2016). *Learning and behavior* (8th ed.). London: Routledge.

McKenna, S.P., & Glendon, A.I. (1985). Occupational first aid training: Decay in cardiopulmonary resuscitation (CPR) skills. *Journal of Occupational Psychology*, *58*, 109–117.

McNally, R.J. (2011). *What is mental illness*? Cambridge, MA: Harvard University Press.

McNeil, J.E., & Warrington, E.K. (1993). Prosopagnosia: A face-specific disorder. *Quarterly Journal of Experimental Psychology*, *46A*, 1–10.

Mehler, J., Jusczyk, P., Lambertz, G., Halsted, N., Bertoncini, J., & Amiel-Tison, C. (1988). A precursor of language acquisition in young infants. *Cognition*, *29*, 143–178.

Milgram, S. (1963). Behavioral study of obedience. *The Journal of Abnormal and Social Psychology*, *67*, 371–378.

Mischel, W., Shoda, Y., & Rodriguez, M.L. (1989). Delay of gratification in children. *Science*, *244*(4907), 933–938.

Moffitt, T.E., Arseneault, L., Belsky, D., Dickson, N., Hancox, R.J., Harrington, H., . . . Sears, M.R. (2011). A gradient of childhood self-control predicts health, wealth, and public safety. *Proceedings of the National Academy of Sciences*, *108*, 2693–2698.

Montgomery, G.H., & Kirsch, I. (1997). Classical conditioning and the placebo effect. *Pain*, *72*, 107–113.

Moser, E.I., Moser, M.B., & McNaughton, B.L. (2017). Spatial representation in the hippocampal formation: A history. *Nature Neuroscience, 20*, 1448–1464.

Murray, C. (2002). IQ and income inequality in a sample of sibling pairs from advantaged family backgrounds. *American Economic Review, 92*, 339–343.

Nisbett, R.E. (2009). *Intelligence and how to get it*. New York, NY: W. W. Norton.

Nissen-Lie, H.A., Monsen, J.T., & Rønnestad, M.H. (2010). Therapist predictors of early patient-rated working alliance: A multilevel approach. *Psychotherapy Research, 20*, 627–646.

Norenzayan, A., & Heine, S.J. (2005). Psychological universals: What are they and how can we know? *Psychological Bulletin, 131*, 763–784.

Oberman, L.M., Hubbard, E.M., McCleery, J.P., Altschuler, E.L., Ramachandran, V.S., & Pineda, J.A. (2005). EEG evidence for mirror neuron dysfunction in autism spectrum disorders. *Cognitive Brain Research, 24*, 190–198.

Owen, A.M., Coleman, M.R., Boly, M., Davis, M.H., Laureys, S., & Pickard, J.D. (2006). Detecting awareness in the vegetative state. *Science, 313*(5792), 1402.

Oyserman, D. (2015). *Pathways to success through identity-based motivation*. New York, NY: Oxford University Press.

Pascalis, O., de Haan, M., & Nelson, C.A. (2002). Is face processing species-specific during the first year of life? *Science, 296*(5571), 1321–1323.

Pascual-Leone, J. (1987). Organismic processes for neo-Piagetian theories: A dialectical causal account of cognitive development. *International Journal of Psychology, 22*, 531–570.

Pavlov, I.P. (1927). *Conditioned reflexes: A study of the physiological activity of the cerebral cortex* (G.V. Anrep, Trans.). Oxford: Oxford University Press.

Pittenger, D.J. (2005). Cautionary comments regarding the Myers-Briggs Type Indicator. *Consulting Psychology Journal: Practice and Research, 57*, 210–221.

Plath, S. (1971). *The bell jar*. New York, NY: Harper & Row.

Protzko, J. (2017). Raising IQ among school-aged children: Five meta-analyses and a review of randomized controlled trials. *Developmental Review, 46*, 81–101.

Reber, R. (2016). *Critical feeling: How to use feelings strategically*. Cambridge: Cambridge University Press.

Reber, R., Canning, E.A., & Harackiewicz, J.M. (2018). Personalized education to increase interest. *Current Directions in Psychological Science, 27*, 449–454.

Reisenzein, R. (1983). The Schachter theory of emotion: Two decades later. *Psychological Bulletin, 94*, 239–264.

Rogers, C.R. (1951). *Client-centered therapy: Its current practice, implications, and theory*. Oxford: Houghton Mifflin.

Rosenhan, D. (1973). On being sane in insane places. *Science, 179*(4070), 250–258.

Rosenthal, R. (1990). How are we doing in soft psychology? *American Psychologist, 45*, 775–777.

Rosenthal, R., & Rubin, D.B. (1982). A simple, general purpose display of magnitude of experimental effect. *Journal of Educational Psychology, 74*, 166–169.

Rosenzweig, S. (1936). Some implicit common factors in diverse methods of psychotherapy. *American Journal of Orthopsychiatry, 6*, 412–415.

Ross, M., & Sicoly, F. (1979). Egocentric biases in availability and attribution. *Journal of Personality and Social Psychology, 37*, 322–336.

Rothbart, M.K. (2007). Temperament, development, and personality. *Current Directions in Psychological Science, 16*, 207–212.

Rozin, P. (2006). Domain denigration and process preference in academic psychology. *Perspectives on Psychological Science, 1*, 365–376.

Russell, J.A. (2003). Core affect and the psychological construction of emotion. *Psychological Review, 110*, 145–172.

Schachter, S.S., & Singer, J.E. (1962). Cognitive, social, and physiological determinants of emotional state. *Psychological Review, 69*, 379–399.

Scherer, K.R. (1984). On the nature and function of emotion: A component process approach. In P. Ekman (Ed.), *Approaches to emotion*. Hillsdale, NJ: Erlbaum.

Schmidt, F.L., & Hunter, J. (2004). General mental ability in the world of work: Occupational attainment and job performance. *Journal of Personality and Social Psychology, 86*, 162–173.

Schwarz, N. (1998). Accessible content and accessibility experiences: The interplay of declarative and experiential information in judgment. *Personality and Social Psychology Review, 2*, 87–99.

Scoville, W.B., & Milner, B. (1957). Loss of recent memory after bilateral hippocampal lesions. *Journal of Neurology, Neurosurgery, and Psychiatry*, *20*, 11–21.

Sherif, M., Harvey, O.J., White, B.J., Hood, W., & Sherif, C. W. (1961). *Intergroup conflict and cooperation: The Robbers Cave experiment*. Norman, OK: University Book Exchange.

Simon, H.A. (1990). Invariants of human behavior. *Annual Review of Psychology*, *41*, 1–20.

Smith, M.L., & Glass, G.V. (1977). Meta-analysis of psychotherapy outcome studies. *American Psychologist*, *32*, 752–760.

Snyder, M., Tanke, E.D., & Berscheid, E. (1977). Social perception and interpersonal behavior: On the self-fulfilling nature of social stereotypes. *Journal of Personality and Social Psychology*, *35*, 656–666.

Soto, C.J., & John, O.P. (2017). The next Big Five Inventory (BFI-2): Developing and assessing a hierarchical model with 15 facets to enhance bandwidth, fidelity, and predictive power. *Journal of Personality and Social Psychology*, *113*, 117–143.

Soto, C.J., John, O.P., Gosling, S.D., & Potter, J. (2011). Age differences in personality traits from 10 to 65: Big Five domains and facets in a large cross-sectional sample. *Journal of Personality and Social Psychology*, *100*, 330–348.

Speisman, J.C., Lazarus, R.S., Mordkoef, A., & Davison, L. (1964). Experimental reduction of stress based on ego-defense theory. *Journal of Abnormal and Social Psychology*, *68*, 367–380.

Spitz, R.A. (1945). Hospitalism: An inquiry into the genesis of psychiatric conditions in early childhood. *The Psychoanalytic Study of the Child*, *1*, 53–74.

Sternberg, R.J. (1986). A triangular theory of love. *Psychological Review*, *93*, 119–135.

Styron, W. (1990). *Darkness visible: A memoir of madness*. New York, NY: Random House.

Tanaka, J.W., & Farah, M.J. (1993). Parts and wholes in face recognition. *Quarterly Journal of Experimental Psychology*, *46A*, 225–245.

Thorndike, E.L. (1898). Animal intelligence: An experimental study of the associative processes in animals. *The Psychological Review: Monograph Supplements*, *2*(4).

Thurstone, L.L. (1938). Primary mental abilities. *Psychometric Monographs*, *1*.

Tolman, E.C. (1948). Cognitive maps in rats and men. *Psychological Review*, *55*, 189–208.

Trahan, L., Stuebing, K.K., Hiscock, M.K., & Fletcher, J.M. (2014). The Flynn effect: A meta-analysis. *Psychological Bulletin*, *140*, 1332–1360.

Turkheimer, E., Haley, A., Waldron, M., D'Onofrio, B., & Gottesman, I.I. (2003). Socioeconomic status modifies heritability of IQ in young children. *Psychological Science*, *14*, 623–628.

Tversky, A., & Kahneman, D. (1973). Availability: A heuristic for judging frequency and probability. *Cognitive Psychology*, *5*, 207–232.

Tversky, A., & Kahneman, D. (1974). Judgment under uncertainty: Heuristics and biases. *Science*, *185*(4157), 1124–1131.

Van der Horst, F.C.P. (2011). *John Bowlby – From psychoanalysis to ethology: Unraveling the roots of attachment theory*. Chichester: Wiley.

Wakefield, J.C. (2016). Diagnostic issues and controversies in DSM-5: Return of the false positives problem. *Annual Review of Clinical Psychology*, *12*, 105–132.

Wampold, B.E., & Imel, Z.E. (2015). *The great psychotherapy debate: The evidence for what makes psychotherapy work*. New York, NY: Routledge.

Wason, P.C. (1960). On the failure to eliminate hypotheses in a conceptual task. *Quarterly Journal of Experimental Psychology*, *12*, 129–140.

Watson, J.B. (1945/1924). *Behaviorism*. London: Kegan Paul, Trench, Trubner.

Watson, J.B., & Rayner, R. (1920). Conditioned emotional reactions. *Journal of Experimental Psychology*, *3*, 1–14.

Wechsler, D. (1944). *The measurement of adult intelligence* (3rd ed.). Baltimore, MD: Williams & Wilkins.

Weiner, B. (1979). A theory of motivation for some classroom experiences. *Journal of Educational Psychology*, *71*, 3–25.

Wellman, H.M., & Gelman, S.A. (1992). Cognitive development: Foundational theories of core domains. *Annual Review of Psychology*, *43*, 337–375.

Willis, J., & Todorov, A. (2006). First impressions: Making up your mind after a 100-ms exposure to a face. *Psychological Science*, *17*, 592–598.

Wimmer, H., & Perner, J. (1983). Beliefs about beliefs: Representation and constraining function of wrong beliefs in young children's understanding of deception. *Cognition, 13*, 103–128.

Wixted, J.T., & Wells, G.L. (2017). The relationship between eyewitness confidence and identification accuracy: A new synthesis. *Psychological Science in the Public Interest, 18*, 10–65.

Wolpe, J. (1973). *The practice of behavior therapy* (2nd ed.). Oxford: Pergamon.

INDEX

Manufactured by Amazon.ca
Bolton, ON